TALKS MY FATHER NEVER HAD WITH ME

(Helping The Young Male Make It To Adulthood)

Volume I

Dr. Harold D. Davis

KJAC Publishing

P.O. Box 111
Champaign, Illinois 61824
Additional books may be ordered by writing the above
address or calling 1-800-268-5861.

Cover Design by Carlton Bruett
Left: Greg Bunch and son Lawson
Right: Johnnie Lee Harris and son Kevin
Drawings by Chris Evans

www.kjac-publishing.com   staff@kjac-publishing.com

CONTENTS

1. How To Meet Strangers 3
2. Expectations With An Example 7
3. Self-Discipline 11
4. The Power of A Positive Attitude 17
5. Things You Can't Change 23
6. Understanding How I Learn 29
7. Defeated By Rejection 35
8. Fools And Foolish Behavior 39
9. Loyalty: What is it? Who needs it? 45
10. Getting Even 49
11. Grades! (Are they important?) 55
12. They Made Me MAD! (Controlling your anger) 61
13. Trash Talking (Is It Worth It?) 67
14. Every Boy Needs A Man In His Face 73
15. My Teacher, My Friend 77
16. TV and Reality 83
17. Family Equals Joy And Pain 89
18. Girls (Sugar And Spice And Everything Nice) .. 95
19. I Got Busted And I Didn't Do It! 101
20. Stupid Stuff 107
21. Who Do You Act Like? 111
22. Moral Restraints 115
23. How To Change Your Bad Habits 119
24. Peach People (Understanding Different Races) 127
25. I Will Stay In My Seat 133
26. Three Kinds Of Dumb 137
27. What I'm Gonna Be When I Grow Up ... 143
28. The Truth About The Truth 149
29. Peer Pressure 153

1. How To Meet Strangers

You are beginning a relationship with a man who has agreed to spend some time with you and share some of his wisdom with you. You are making a first impression today. A first impression is what people think about you the first time they meet you. First impressions are important because they cannot be repeated. You do not know this man, who has agreed to mentor you and just like all men you meet you will need to make a good first impression and get to know him. How do you learn something about a man when you first meet him? Well, the first thing you should do when you meet a stranger is introduce yourself. This is done by shaking the man's hand and looking him in the eye. It has been said that to look into a man's eye is to look into his soul.

When you shake a man's hand, you can learn a little bit about him based on how hard he squeezes your hand, how fast he shakes it and how long he holds on. In our American culture, you should be concerned when a man will not look you in the eye. This is a sign that either he has something to hide or he does not feel good about himself. Another reason you should look him in the eye is that only really good liars can look you in the eye and lie to you.

You can also learn about a man by the clothes he wears. Some men wear suits and ties. Other men wear blue jeans. Our society gives a lot of respect to men who wear suits and ties. Some days I wear a suit and tie and some days I wear blue jeans. When I go in a store with a suit on, people give me more respect than when I go in a store with blue jeans on. Some men wear suits to impress others and other men wear suits because they like them. It is a fact that the clothes we wear affect how others view us.

Another thing to consider when meeting a stranger is the manner in which he speaks to you. For example, if you meet a stranger and he just says "hi," you can tell that he may not be very excited about meeting you or that he is not much of a talker. On the other hand, if he says: "Hello, my name is David. What is your name?," you can see that he is showing an interest in getting to know you.

I suggest that when you meet a new person, you take the lead. Shake the person's hand, look the person in the eye and say "Hello, my name is ___. It is a pleasure to meet you." This makes a good first impression. The person that you are meeting thinks that you are a smart person and a nice person. This is good for you.

Some men are "people people" and they love meeting strangers and getting to know them. Usually they will give you a greeting when you meet them. Other people are not very interested in meeting new people. They prefer to be alone and work with machines.

These men will say "hello" to you and never really look at you very much.

How would you like to present yourself when you meet new people? Would you like them to see you as a "people person" who likes to meet new people or would you like for them to see you as a "non-people person" who prefers machines and not people?

What do you think about your mentor, this man that you have just met? How do you see him? What have you figured out about him in this short time since you have met him? Do you feel that he is a "people person" or would he work well with machines? Does he wear a suit or does he dress casually? Have you shaken his hand? If so, how did he do? I want to challenge you to analyze your first impression of him and remember it. Later, after you get to know him better you can go back and see if your analysis of him was right. If you learn how to do this well, it will help you in the future as you meet new people.

Wisdom (to be discussed with your mentor)

If a man be gracious and courteous to strangers, it shows he is a citizen of the world, and that his heart is no island cut off from other lands, but a continent that joins them.
ESSAYS 1625, OF GOODNESS AND GOODNESS OF NATURE

When one is a stranger to oneself then one is estranged from others too. ANNE MORROW LINDBERGH

Ants and savages put strangers to death.
BERTRAND RUSSELL

There are...two kinds of people in this world, those who long to be understood and those who long to be misunderstood. It is the irony of life that neither is gratified. CARL VAN VECHTEN

Whoever lives at a different end of town from me, I look upon as persons out of the world, and only myself and the scene about me to be in it.
JONATHAN SWIFT

You have only one chance to make a first impression. Make it count. MARKITA ANDREWS

The only justification for ever looking down on somebody is to pick them up. JESSE JACKSON

When you face a crisis, you know who your true friends are. EARVIN "MAGIC" JOHNSON

2. Expectations With An Example

My mother has always encouraged me to be my best. She always told me that I could do whatever I wanted to do. My mom had high expectations of me. I have learned that it is easier to reach your goals when you have an example to follow. All of my life I have looked for men to be good examples for me. We all do better when we have an example. An example is someone that we can imitate and copy. Children are great imitators; they can do almost anything that they see other children or adults do.

Not too long ago, there was a famous basketball player who stuck his tongue out when he played. I don't know why he stuck his tongue out, he just did it. Before too long, kids all across America were playing basketball and sticking their tongues out. I guess the kids stuck their tongues out because of the example that had been set.

Adults in our society have expectations of you and all young people, especially boys. They expect you to talk politely, be considerate, work very hard and prepare yourselves to be the future rulers of this country. Those are the expectations. If adults have these expectations of you, then they must be prepared to provide examples for you to follow. In other words, it is easier to do what is expected of you when you watch someone else do it.

When I take a minute to think about my youth, I remember that there were always adults who had expectations of me. My mother had great expectations of me. She would often tell me: "You can do it son, you can do it!" It didn't matter what it was. She would tell me that I could do it. Now that I am grown I realize that my mom's expectations encouraged me. Let me ask you a question: When someone tells you that they believe that you can do "it," whatever "it" is, how does that make you feel? For me, it motivated me and made me really want to accomplish what they believed that I could do. A very important thing to remember when someone has high expectations of you is to immediately find someone to watch who has already accomplished what you are trying to do.

My mom was not my example of a businessman, musician or baseball player. Other people served as those examples. I had to find someone to be an example in every area that I wanted to excel in. So, it is possible that your mom, dad or friend can have high expectations of you, but another person can be your example to help you reach those goals.

My dad also had high expectations of me and he was the example for me in many areas, but there were other men who knew more about certain things than my dad did. In those areas I listened to them and learned from them. It is important to remember that all men have areas where they are strong and areas where they are weak. All men have areas where they know a lot and other areas where they don't know anything.

I think that because of your age, you should work very hard on meeting the expectations of your parents, teachers and mentors. Studying hard in school is the number one job for young people. The lessons that you learn in school will help you meet the challenges of the future. Remember, when you are challenged to learn something new that may be difficult and challenging, find an example to follow. Learn to ask for help when you need help finding an example. Remember that healthy adults enjoy helping young people who are serious about improving themselves.

Wisdom (to be discussed with your mentor)

People seldom improve when they have no model but themselves to copy after. OLIVER GOLDSMITH

Example is the school of mankind, and they will learn at no other. EDMUND BURKE

A good example is the best sermon. THOMAS FULLER
It is the true nature of mankind to learn from mistakes, not from example. FRED HOYLE

There is a difference between imitating a good man and counterfeiting him. BENJAMIN FRANKLIN

We are all too quick to imitate depraved examples.
JUVENAL

Lives of great men all remind us, We can make our lives sublime, And, departing, leave behind us Footprints on the sands of time. LONGFELLOW

Success always leaves footprints.
BOOKER T. WASHINGTON

3. Self-Discipline

I have worked hard to have self-discipline in my life. Self-discipline is the ability to do the right thing at the right time, like study, clean up your room or turn your homework in on time. When I was a kid, there was a family in our neighborhood named the Harrisons. They were very different from most of the other families because their kids were very disciplined. Their parents did not let them spend all day at the playground. They made them come in the house before it was dark. We would often tease them and call them babies and momma's boys because they could not hang out like the rest of the boys.

What we did not know was that while these kids were in the house, they were working on their homework and learning how to have discipline in their lives. They learned at an early age that there is a time to play and there is a time to work. Many kids and adults never learn the difference between the two. Well, the Harrisons learned at a early age that you must do the right thing at the right time. They did play and have fun, but they did it at the right time and at the right place. They did not horse around in school and get in trouble. They always did their work well and always had their homework in on time.

As we grew older, entered high school and college, we noticed that the Harrison boys were always the smartest kids in class. They took all of the hard classes like algebra, calculus, and advanced English, and they did well in them. Now that they are grown, they are engineers with good jobs and they make good money. So, who is laughing now? Who is having fun now? Who gets to play now?!

It is very unfortunate that many kids spend too much time playing and not enough time preparing for their future. If you plan to grow up, you will need a job, a house to live in and food to eat. Your parents will not be around to take care of you forever. If you are wise, you will do like the Harrisons did. They worked when it was time to work and they played when it was time to play, and in the end they were ready for their future.

When a boy understands that the future is coming, he will see the need to be disciplined. Many stories are designed to teach children about discipline. For example, think of the three little pigs. If you remember, the first two pigs were almost eaten by the wolf because they were lazy and not disciplined. Parents work hard to teach their children discipline because parents know that if their children don't learn discipline, they will not be successful in life.

Many boys who do not learn discipline early in life end up in prison or worse. Today, I work with adults who partied all of the time while they were young and they never had discipline. When I was in school,

I met people who wanted to party more than they wanted to study. They suffer now as a result of their choices when there were young. Self-discipline in the life of a child is worth more than a million dollars because **if you have discipline you can always make money.**

One good thing about the Harrison family is that they had parents to make them come inside and work. Many kids today don't have parents to make them do right. What are these kids supposed to do? Well, they are supposed to make themselves do right. It works this way. When you know that it is time for you to be disciplined and there is no one there to discipline you, you should talk to yourself and say something like this: "I know that it is time for me to go in the house and study. I also know that if I don't do this, I will not be prepared for class tomorrow. I am going to do what is right and go to my room and do my homework." I want you to know that it is alright to talk to yourself when you are telling yourself to do something good.

What about you? Are you disciplined? Do you do the right thing at the right time? The results of your discipline will show up when you become an adult, just like in the Harrison family.

Wisdom (to be discussed with your mentor)

Take off the strong cord of discipline and morality and you will be an old man before your twenties are past. Preserve these forces. Do not burn them out in idleness or crime. PRESIDENT GARFIELD

Discipline is the soul of an army. It makes small numbers formidable; procures success to the weak, and esteem, to all. LETTER OF INSTRUCTIONS TO THE CAPTAINS OF VIRGINIA REGIMENTS (July 29, 1759)

Perhaps the most valuable result of all education is the ability to make yourself do the thing you have to do, when it ought to be done, whether you like it or not. WALTER BAGEHOT

Children have to be educated, but they have also to be left to educate themselves. ABBE' DIMNET

It is better to be slow-tempered than famous; it is better to have self-control than to control an army. PROVERBS 16:32

He who conquers others is strong; He who conquers himself is mighty. LAO-TZU

He that would govern others, first should be Master of himself. PHILIP MASSINGER

He is most powerful who has power over himself.
SENECA

He who is allowed to do as he likes will soon run his head into a brick wall out of sheer frustration.
ROBERT MUSIL

You will never develop discipline until you start with small pieces. B. J. TATUM

Notes:_____

_____

_____

_____

_____

_____

_____

_____

_____

_____

_____

_____

_____

_____

4. The Power Of A Positive Attitude

I never will forget Mrs. Grey's favorite words when a boy was misbehaving in her class. She would walk up to the boy, get very close to his face and say: "Young man, you need to change your attitude!" This is what she would tell the boys in her class when they would frown, pout, throw things and display bad behavior or a bad attitude. Your attitude is your state of mind. It can be pleasant, good and positive or it can be unpleasant, bad and negative. Adults hate it when kids have bad attitudes. A bad attitude can be very unpleasant to the people around you and it can turn others off.

I had a girlfriend once who had a bad attitude. I thought she was cute and she did look good on the outside, but on the inside she had a stinky attitude. A good attitude can be worth more than a million dollars because people like kids with good attitudes. When I was a kid, my dad would knock me out if my attitude turned stinky. Today, adults do not knock kids out. They just ignore and avoid them. To be ignored is worse than being knocked out. When adults ignore kids with bad attitudes, the attitude becomes the real enemy that needs to be dealt with.

A bad attitude will cause you to be the last one considered when it is time to pick kids for the fun things in life. A bad attitude is when something is stinking on the inside and the person tries to pour it

17

out on everyone around him. Mrs. Grey would show her disgust with us boys when we had a bad attitude and we would miss out on many fun activities. Now that I am grown, I understand why adults hate bad attitudes in kids. I always encourage kids to have good attitudes because a good attitude will open many doors for you. Let's look at some of the reasons you should work on having a good attitude.

1. A bad attitude only hurts you. It is a childish mistake to believe that your bad attitude is punishing someone else. Your bad attitude *always* hurts you more than it hurts other people. Your bad attitude separates you from people who could and would help you. Unfortunately, I have seen young people with attitudes suffer many things and not know why. I can remember when a 5-year-old kid walked up to his mom and said: "If you don't let me go outside and play, I am going to hold my breath until I die!" The kid then held his breath until he turned red and eventually he decided to breathe. The kid was trying to punish the parent by hurting himself. This is the same thing that happens when an older person has a bad attitude. It only hurts you and you look very foolish holding your breath.

2. A bad attitude may indicate that you have other problems. Usually when kids have a bad attitude, they are mad at someone about something that person did. Many times it is their father or mother that they are mad at. What the child does not realize is that when he has a bad attitude in school because he is mad at someone at home, it is misdirected anger. Misdirected anger is when you are mad at the people who didn't do anything to you. When a kid yells at Jennifer when David is the one who hit him that is misdirected anger. If you must have a bad attitude, have it with the people who hurt you and not with others who are trying to help you. The mature thing to do is to learn not to misdirect your anger.

3. Some kids have bad attitudes because they feel that no one loves them. Some kids have been hurt by adults who should have loved them, so they now are mean to all adults who would be kind to them because they fear that another adult will hurt them. They have a bad attitude because they don't want anyone to get close enough to show them love. This defensive tactic actually makes it hard for adults to get close to them and be their friend.

4. Some kids have bad attitudes because their family and friends have bad attitudes. It is hard to be loving and kind when everyone around you is bitter and negative. It is hard to do, but it can be done. I have met some wonderful young people who have come out of bitter homes. They made up their minds that they were not going to be bitter but work on getting better.

There is an old saying that your attitude will determine your altitude. I believe that this is true because life must be lived around other people. Other people will pick up on your attitude very quickly, so a good attitude will do wonders to help you get ahead in life and a bad attitude can really hold you back. The choice is yours. You can choose to work toward having a good attitude or you can just have a stinky attitude and live with the results. What will it be?

Wisdom (to be discussed with your mentor)

A negative attitude is a true handicap.
THE IMPOSSIBLE DREAM, 1986

Persistence and a positive attitude are necessary ingredients for any successful venture. ANONYMOUS

It is impossible for a people to rise above their aspirations. If we think we cannot we most certainly cannot. Our greatest enemy is our defeatist attitude.
ROBERT WILLIAMS

Only those who dare to fail greatly can ever achieve greatly. ROBERT F. KENNEDY

The secret to success is to learn to accept the impossible, to do without the indispensable, and to bear the intolerable. NELSON MANDELA

No one knows less than the person who knows it all.

I don't understand it. People are always saying that I've got an attitude. WHOOPI GOLDBERG

I've benefited from many scholarships. A number of people paid a lot of dues for me to do what I do. I feel it's my responsibility to give back. WYNTON MARSALIS

Notes:_____

_____

_____

_____

_____

_____

_____

_____

_____

_____

_____

_____

_____

_____

5. Things You Can't Change

One of the joys of being young is that you have the rest of your life to overcome any problem or struggle that you face. I can remember that as a kid, I did not learn how to swim. I had always wanted to learn how to swim, but I was afraid of water because I almost drowned when I was six years old. Not long ago, I put my mind to it and swam for the first time in my life.

What's exciting about this story is that there was something that I couldn't do, something I was afraid of, but I learned how to do it. I am excited about the things that I can change in my life, but I also realize that there are many things in life that no one can change.

One of the keys to being successful is learning how to deal with the things you can't change. There are two types of problems in life: the kind that you can change and the kind that you can't change. Many people waste many years of their lives trying to change things that will never change. You can't change the color of your skin or your sex. You can't change where you were born or who your parents are or how tall you are. Accepting these unchangeable things as facts of life is very important.

It is also very important to work hard to change the things you can change. Just as I overcame my fear of swimming, there are things you need to overcome. Elementary school is a very important time in life. It is a time when many boys develop the attitude of a winner or a loser. I can remember a boy in my 4th grade class named Clinton. Clinton became a loser in the 4th grade because he failed a geography test and decided that he would never be any good in geography or any other class. From that day on, Clinton never really tried very hard to do well in school.

Clinton's problem was that he did not choose to change the things that he could change. It takes guts to face a problem and decide to work to change it. Let me share some steps you can take to challenge and change the problems that you can change.

1. Identify the problem. If you are making poor grades, suffering with behavior problems or forget to take baths, your problem is easy to identify. A simple change of behavior is all that is needed. Listen to other people who care about you. They will identify areas in your life that you need to work on. Even critics can give good advice every now and then.

2. Determine if this is a problem that can be changed. Remember that there are some problems that can't be changed for reasons beyond your control. One key thing to remember is that you can't change other people. If you like a girl and she does not like you, you can't change that; but you can change the way you feel about her.

3. Share with an adult that you want to change and get some advice from them. A secret that most adults will not tell you is that they are just like you. They have had many problems that they have tried to change and they found out that some problems they could change and others they could not change. They have experience with problems and a lot of wisdom and advice to share with you as you face the problems in your life.

4. Start doing the things you need to do to bring about the change. Think about this: If you act a certain way, you will begin to think a certain way. You can develop new habits by doing something every day, the same way. Before long, you will have a new habit. Habits are formed by doing something over and over.

5. Always celebrate your success. A reward is always in order when a task is completed successfully. Learn early in life to reward yourself when you accomplish a goal. This reward may simply be telling yourself out loud in private that you did well. The reward may be more significant like a trip to your favorite fast food restaurant.

For the rest of your life, you will be challenged with problems. Decide to face them head on! Remember to seek the advice and encouragement of others as you seek to make changes in your life. Don't forget to celebrate when you successfully eliminate a bad habit.

One of the greatest things that you can *always* change is your attitude. If you have a bad attitude you can choose to change it by deciding to have a good attitude. When we are motivated we can choose to change our attitudes. I know this is true because not too long ago I was with three boys and one of them had a bad attitude. We had planned to go out for a burger on this day and I told him that if he didn't change his attitude he would not go. An amazing thing happened. He immediately took the frown off of his face and began smiling; he chose to change his attitude. Remember that you can change your attitude if you want to, but you can't change the attitude of others.

Are you ready to start changing the things you can change, identifying and dealing wisely with the things you can't change? Good luck.

Wisdom (to be discussed with your mentor)

When it comes to changes, people like only those they make themselves. FRENCH PROVERB

None but a fool worries about things he cannot influence. SAMUEL JOHNSON

Change is not made without inconvenience, even from worse to better. RICHARD HOOKER

All things must change to something new, to something strange. HENRY WADSWORTH LONGFELLOW

Every new adjustment is a crisis in self-esteem. ERIC HOFFER

The world hates change, yet it is the only thing that has brought progress. CHARLES F. KETTERING

Everyone thinks of changing the world, but no one thinks of changing himself. LEO TOLSTOY

God grant me the serenity to accept the things that can't be changed, the courage to change the things I can and the wisdom to know the difference. REINHOLD NIEBUHR

A wise man changes his mind sometimes, a fool never PROVERB

It takes twenty-one years to be twenty-one. REGGIE JACKSON

Notes:_____

_____

_____

_____

_____

_____

_____

_____

_____

_____

_____

_____

_____

_____

6. Understanding How I Learn

I enjoy being an adult because I now understand why so many subjects really bothered me in elementary school. To tell the truth, I was not the smartest kid in the class. I struggled with math, science, geography and spelling. I really thought that I was just a dumb kid. It was not until I went to college to be a teacher that I learned that there are different ways to learn.

You see, in every classroom there are different learning styles. For example, some people can see something and remember it. If they see it on the board, in a book, or on TV they can remember it. These people are called visual learners. They can see something and the information goes straight to the brain and is stored. Other people can hear something and they have it. If the teacher says it, they hear it on a tape, or they hear it from a friend, they can remember it. These people are called auditory learners (auditory means hearing).

There are still other kids who must touch something to learn it. I believe that this is the kind of kid that I was in school. This kid is called the tactile (touch) learner. Many times tactile learners have difficulty because it is difficult to touch math or a story that you are reading in a book. The teacher may not take enough time to allow every child to touch the subject matter. There are still other kids who learn through a combination of the three. The most important thing is for you to figure out early in life how you learn. Do you understand your learning style? Are you a visual learner, a auditory learner or a tactile learner?

Babies learn about things by putting things in their mouth and tasting them. I hope you don't do that any more. It is very important to discover your learning style so that you can begin to concentrate on using it to get the best possible grades. Remember that we all learn differently and that no one learning style is better than the others. The important thing is to discover how you learn and then become very good at mastering it.

Be sure to eliminate any obstacles that would prohibit you from learning. My son was having trouble getting his assignments in school. We had him tested and learned that he needed glasses. There are other children who have been labeled learning disabled when the only thing wrong was they had a hearing problem. If you feel that there is a physical problem holding you back, please be sure to talk to your teacher about it.

I am excited to understand how I learn and I am working on mastering my learning style. Also it is very important for me to continue to develop the other styles that are not natural to me. For example, I learn better when I read and then write what I have read. If I don't write it, most of the time I don't remember it. I am now working on becoming stronger in just reading the material one time and then knowing it. This is a challenge for me which I am enjoying very much.

You should seek to learn from people who have learning styles that are different than yours. For example, my wife has a learning style that is different than mine. I watch how she works her learning system and I try to imitate her. This has helped me develop in other areas. Never be intimidated by how you learn, because if you really master your learning style you will be able to go on and accomplish many great things.

Very often people around us can tell us a lot about ourselves. Talk to your teacher to see if she understands your learning style. Ask him/her if they would help you master your learning style. Also talk to parents and other adults who have watched you for some time. They can be very helpful. I predict that if you start working to understand your learning style that your grades will improve this year and you will be proud of how smart you really are.

Wisdom (to be discussed with your mentor)

All our talents increase in the using, and every faculty both good and bad, strengthens by exercise.
ANNE BRONTE

What we have to learn to do, we learn by doing.
ARISTOTLE

Learning is by nature curiosity . . . prying into everything, reluctant to leave anything, material or immaterial unexplained. PHILO

Don't measure yourself by what you have accomplished, but by what you should have accomplished with your ability. BEN CHAVIS

Disabilities can sometimes be definitions. You can think of yourself in terms of what you can't do and never realize the possibilities of what you can do.
BONNIE ST. JOHN

Start where you are with what you have, knowing that what you have is plenty enough. BOOKER T. WASHINGTON

Great opportunities come to those who make the most of small ones. DEMPSEY TRAVIS

We learn from failure much more than from success.
JOHN H. JOHNSON

Notes:_____

_____

_____

_____

_____

_____

_____

_____

_____

_____

_____

_____

_____

_____

7. Defeated By Rejection

Not too long ago, I had to take a trip on an airplane. As I approached the plane, I extended my hand to the flight attendant to shake her hand. She stood there with her hands folded in front of her and she refused to shake my hand. She rejected me! I experienced a mild form of rejection. Maybe she thought that I had not washed my hands, so she did not want to shake my hand. Whatever the reason, she rejected me.

At first I became angry at the fact that she did not want to shake my hand. I said to myself: "I can't believe that she thinks she is better than I am!" Then I began to ask myself: "What is wrong with me? Do I have bad breath? Is it because I am a man, is it because I am Black?" When we are rejected we always want to know why. As I sat in my seat on the plane I began to realize how this woman had affected me. I had actually allowed her to make me to feel defeated and angry. Once I realized what had happened, I determined to get myself together and not let her rejection affect me.

Rejection is a powerful force that all of us encounter at one time or another. The most common form of rejection is when a girl rejects a boy who wants to be her boyfriend. I can remember when I was 12 and I asked Gilta (a cute girl in my neighborhood) to go to the movie with me. She told me no and I felt rejected. She then told me that she would go with me if I took two of her friends also. Like a dummy, I did it. People do many dumb things to keep from being rejected by a date. When a girl kicks a guy to the curb and goes on to someone else, the boy is usually devastated. Millions of love songs have been written about being rejected by a someone.

Another form of rejection is the rejection of peers. In school I was always rejected by Freddie, who was the most athletic boy in the school. He never picked me to be on his dodge ball team. I told people that it didn't bother me, but deep down inside I was angry every time it happened. I said to myself: "Forget Freddie!" and I played on the losing team. I also felt rejected by the rich kids who would not talk to me. They would not talk to me because they were rich and by the smart kids who only talked to other smart kids. It was rough enduring the rejection of the other kids in school.

It is important to realize that people who reject others only do so because they don't feel good about themselves. People who don't feel good about themselves need to reject other kids because it helps them feel better about themselves. It is a primitive human behavior to put another person down so that you can feel better. I watch little children do it all of the time. One kid will tell another kid: "I got three pieces of candy, you only got two." The attempt to show that I am better than you are is a human behavior that is not good.

I can remember when Freddie rejected Walter and refused to let him play on his team. Later that same day I saw Walter reject another kid the same way Freddie did him. Actually when most people reject you it is because they need to feel better about themselves. You need to always remember that when you are rejected by a person, it is just one person's opinion.

The key to all of this is to remember not to let the rejection affect you or defeat you. Too many kids in school feel rejected because they received a low grade on a test or they failed a subject. Other kids feel bad and rejected because they do not play sports well. Some kids feel rejected because someone told them they did not want to be their friend. To feel rejected because of what someone else says about you is to hurt yourself. It is not what the other person says about you but what you feel about yourself.

Well, what about you? Have you been defeated by rejection? Have you rejected other kids and made them feel bad? It is a terrible thing to reject kids and make them feel bad for any reason at all. The proper thing to do is to remember how it feels to be rejected before you reject someone else. If we all considered how bad it felt, we would think before we rejected others.

Wisdom (to be discussed with your mentor)

No one can figure out your worth but you.
PEARL BAILEY

Fall seven times, stand up eight.   JAPANESE PROVERB

Do not be afraid of defeat. You are never so near to victory as when defeated in a good cause.
HENRY WARD BEECHER

To lose is to learn.   ANONYMOUS

What is defeat? Nothing but education, nothing but the first step toward something better.
WENDELL PHILLIPS

And a good rejection slip can be more educational than a mediocre workshop. ANONYMOUS

It is said that Walt Disney didn't get excited about any idea unless all the members of the board resisted it. If even a few were in favor, the idea dimmed for him. the challenge wasn't great enough to spark the energy he knew it would require.
ANONYMOUS

Believe in yourself and your abilities. There are lots of other folks who'll tell you, "It can't be done."
JASMINE GUY

8. Fools and Foolish Behavior

The dictionary describes a fool as a person who has little or no judgement, wisdom or common sense. It is an awful, awful thing to be a fool or to be considered a fool by other people. The problem with most fools is that they don't realize that they are fools. They don't listen to those who would help them understand their situation. It is not a good thing to call someone a fool. You should never do this because no one understands why people act the way they do. It is very sad when a young person acts foolishly.

We need to become aware of and challenge our foolish behaviors. Foolish behavior is behavior that is common to fools. One area where most men have acted foolishly is in the area of female relations. I remember my first date with Gilta. I was in junior high school and she was in high school. I was so nervous that I said and did some foolish things. Boys do many foolish things around girls. It is never too early for a young man to learn how to be wise around women.

People do foolish things because they reject the wisdom of older people. When I was in high school my dad, who was 60 years old, would share wisdom with me. I learned that when I would reject his wisdom, especially as it related to human nature, I would suffer for it. The opposite of foolish behavior is wise behavior. Wisdom usually comes from older men. As I look back over my life, I see that I did some wise things and some foolish things. The wise things were done while I was hanging out with wise older men. The foolish things were done while I was hanging out with foolish young men.

In most schools you can find fools and foolish behavior. I repeat that it is not your job to call them fools, but it is your job to avoid them. Fools can be very dangerous, especially when you mix them with certain things like guns, cars, firecrackers, drugs, a bad attitude, beer, rejection by a girlfriend and on and on.

As young men, you must be very careful to avoid fools and the foolish things that they do. One bad decision in the presence of a fool can cost you your reputation, your health or even your life. I remember one Friday night when I needed a ride home from a football game and I did something stupid. I got in a car with a fool who had been drinking. That was stupid! When I got in the car, he pressed the gas pedal to the floor and was going 75 miles per hour on a residential street. He could have *killed* me! From that day on, I was *very* careful about whom I rode with.

Fools are dangerous because they do things that other people would only think about doing. It is not uncommon for young people to slip and do something foolish. That does not mean that you are a fool. My friend Merrit was a very intelligent person. One Halloween we were walking down the street and he did something very foolish. He took an egg out of his pocket and threw it at an old lady's house. The egg splattered on the front window and the old lady called the police. They took Merrit to jail and they threatened to take me to jail also. My friend realized that he was foolish and later asked the old lady to forgive him. The good thing is that he did not try to blame it on me. Very often fools get other people in trouble.

It is a full-time job for a young person to guard against foolish behavior. One thing that you can do is to have an accountability system. This is when you have people in your life who will challenge you anytime they notice you acting foolishly. Mentors are good for this role. Remember that we can all slip and occasionally do something foolish. It is good to have wise friends around to tell us when we act that way.

You are really in trouble when foolish behavior is a way of life. If you act foolishly *all* the time, ask yourself these questions:

1. Have I been disciplined enough? Much foolish behavior is caused when parents do not discipline their kids. The child begins to think that there will be no consequences for his behavior, so he fears nothing and acts any way he wants to.

2. Do I realize what happens to fools and those who display foolish behavior? One of the things that an adult can do is look back at the foolish kids they went to school with and see how their lives turned out. In most cases it was bad.

3. Do I need attention so badly that I act foolishly to get it? It is a fact that everybody needs attention. The question is: "How do you get the attention that you need?"

There are many reasons why young people act foolish. The most important thing is for you to control your personal behavior. Out of all the millions of persons on this planet, your behavior is the only person's behavior that you can control. What is it going to be? Will you behave foolishly or will you behave wisely?

Wisdom (to be discussed with your mentor)

If fifty million people say a foolish thing, it is still a foolish thing. ANATOLE FRANCE

There are some people that if they don't know, you can't tell 'em. LOUIS ARMSTRONG

A fool's head never whitens. OLD SAYING

A fool's fun is being bad; a wise man's fun is being wise! PROVERBS 10:23

It is no fun to be a rebel's father. PROVERBS 17:21

A fool always finds a bigger fool to admire him. NICHOLAS BOILEAU

The man of few words and settled mind is wise; therefore, even a fool is thought to be wise when he is silent. It pays him to keep his mouth shut. PROVERBS 17:28 TLB

The best way to convince a fool that he is wrong is to let him have his own way. JOSH BILLINGS

Wake up. The hour has come to be more responsible. Change this world by starting with yourself. The world is not going to change until you change. DR. BETTY SHABAZZ

When it comes to food for thought, some of us are on a hunger strike. DICK GREGORY

A person completely wrapped up in himself makes a small package. DENZEL WASHINGTON

Notes:_____

_____

_____

_____

_____

_____

_____

_____

_____

_____

_____

_____

_____

_____

9. Loyalty: (What is it? Who Needs It?)

When I was fifteen years old I was in a band. Actually, I was the leader of the band. All of the boys in the band were about fifteen years old and we were friends. As the leader of the band, I picked the songs we sang, negotiated the contracts for the band to play and paid everybody. I enjoyed being the leader of the band because when everything went well, I got the credit. On the other hand, when things went poorly, I got all of the blame.

My best friend in the band was Jamie. Jamie was the singer and he was my best friend. Friendship is important in a band just like it is in sports. Friends work well together and look out for each other. In other words, friends are loyal to each other. I can remember this one day when I went to practice and a very sad thing happened. As I walked into the room, all of the band members were lined up against the wall looking at me. Jamie, my friend, looked at me and said: "We all quit."

I was stunned, surprised and sad all at the same time. I couldn't believe that my good friend would do this. We had been friends for years. I never expected that this would happen. Well, I left that room with a good understanding of what loyalty was because of how badly I felt. I decided that I was going to be loyal to those who trusted me. I decided that if I needed to leave a situation or break off a friendship, I would do it the right way and not the wrong way.

There is a term that older people use called "burning bridges." They say: "You should never burn bridges." What is meant by this is when people help you in life, they are serving as a bridge that gets you from one place to another. Many young people go over the bridge and then act as if they will never need that bridge again. The fact of the matter is we often need people who have helped us before to help us again. If you treat them badly or act as if you will never need them again, you are burning or destroying the bridge that brought you over and it will be difficult to go back to them for help again. You never know who you will need to help you in the future, so always treat everybody nicely.

Our nation needs a new generation of young men who will be loyal to it. Loyalty is the first cousin to honesty and as never before our nation and communities need honesty. We have businesses that fail because men and women are not loyal to their employers. Marriages are failing because men are not loyal to their wives. Schools are failing because teachers are not loyal to their students and students are not loyal to their teachers. Without loyalty, a nation cannot stand for long because no one can be trusted.

I am challenging you to develop a sense of loyalty in your life. It will be a great asset to your family, boss, community and nation. Loyalty should be extended first to those who helped you when you could not help yourself. It makes me very angry to see a kid sass his mother when she suffered pain to bring him into this world. Boys should be loyal to their mothers because for nine months she was loyal to her child while she carried him in her womb.

Loyalty should also be extended to family members and community members who have contributed and are still contributing to your growth and maturity. I am grateful to all of the loyal soldiers who died fighting for our country. Because of their sacrifice, you and I live in a free nation where we can pursue our dreams.

I am loyal to those who have gone before and I show my loyalty by serving the next generation. When I wrote this book to help boys, I was being loyal to America and to all of the men who have died to keep America a free nation. If you and the boys your age stop being loyal to our American principles of justice and freedom for all, our nation will not last long.

You should seek to be loyal to projects that you begin. Learn how to start something and stick with it until it is completed. The attitude of loyalty to a task will help you be a success in life. Never start a school assignment that you do not finish. Be loyal to your word and complete the tasks that you tell your teacher or parents that you are going to complete. Never begin a task that you do not finish. Be loyal to that task.

I want to encourage you to develop the habit of being loyal to those who love you and sacrificed for you. When young men develop this attitude, it will help our nation stay great and our cities and communities will become better places to live.

Wisdom (to be discussed with your mentor)

Friendship is the only cement that will hold the world together. DUKE ELLINGTON

Where ever you are, be there! B.J. TATUM

A truthful witness never lies; a false witness always lies. PROVERBS 14:5

Without virtue man can have no happiness. BENJAMIN FRANKLIN

Many times we find ourselves turning our backs on our actual friends, that we may go and meet their ideal cousins. HENRY DAVID THOREAU

You cannot be friends upon any other terms than upon the terms of equality. WOODROW WILSON

10. Getting Even

I never will forget the day that it happened. I was riding my new bicycle that I had gotten for Christmas. It was my first time having the bicycle out of the house, and boy, was I proud! This was the best bicycle that I had ever owned and it had everything: a mirror, light, horn, streamers, and saddlebags. It was the Cadillac of bicycles, and I was the proudest of owners.

As I was riding my bicycle through the neighborhood, Lamont saw me on my new bicycle. His eyes got as big as two silver dollars. His mouth dropped open and he said: "Wow, this is a bad bike! Can I ride it?" Well, it was not that I did not want him to ride the bicycle, but I had just gotten it and I was still riding the bicycle. So, I told Lamont, "Not right now," but I said I would let him ride the bike later that day. Lamont did not like this, and he frowned and walked away in a huff.

I continued to ride until my mom called me inside to eat. Well, I did not want to take my bike in the house yet so I set it on the front porch so that I could sit at the dinner table and watch it. As I was eating my mashed potatoes and meat loaf, I kept one eye on my bicycle. As I looked up from taking a bite of meatloaf, I saw a hand on my bike and I noticed that it was falling over. I jumped up from the table and dashed out of the front door just in time to see two things: Lamont's back going around the side of the house and my bike hitting the ground, breaking my rear view mirror.

I was so mad that I wanted to commit murder! I said to myself: "I'm going to kill Lamont!" I wanted to fight him as soon as I could find him, but he hid from me and time passed. I cooled down but I still wanted to GET EVEN. Summertime came and Lamont thought that I had forgotten about what he did, but I hadn't. Then my chance came one day in June. Lamont's parents bought him a new skateboard with wide rubber wheels. Lamont was very happy riding his new skateboard, and he was smiling from ear to ear. I waited patiently for my opportunity to strike and three days later Lamont was distracted by a basketball game that some boys were playing. He left his skate board on his front porch at his house. Nobody was home. Nobody was watching. I thought: "Here is my chance."

I took a pair of pliers out of my pocket, took the nut loose on the front right wheel on Lamont's skateboard, took the wheel off and went home. I stopped along the way to throw the wheel over the hill into the weeds where it would never be found again. Finally! I had gotten even. I was not there to see Lamont's face when he found his skateboard, but I am sure that he was very sad, which made me glad.

The next day I saw Lamont walking past my house with his three wheel skateboard in his hand. Just as I thought, he looked very sad. I went out to talk to him so that I could pretend that I was sorry for what happened. As we talked I learned some things that I had not known before. I learned that Lamont's dad was not well and he had taken the money from his last paycheck to buy Lamont that skateboard. I also learned that because of their financial problems that Lamont was going to have to move and live with an Uncle in Detroit. As Lamont continued to tell me all of his problems, tears began to come into his eyes and all of a sudden I began to feel pretty lousy.

I began to think of how good things were with me at my house and how I had nice things but Lamont did not have all the things that I had; he only had a skateboard. After he finished talking, Lamont walked down the street with his head down and I began to feel tremendous guilt. If I had only known all of this before I took the wheel off of his skateboard, I never would have done it. I never told Lamont what I did, and I never replaced the wheel. What I did do was learn a tremendous lesson: *you can never get even!*

The idea of getting even is misleading. There is no way that you can hurt somebody in the same way and to the same degree that they hurt you. You will always hurt them more or less. There is no such thing as even. When you hurt them more than they hurt you, you are just as guilty as they are for starting it in the first place. Because I am a human being, I do not know what other people are going through or what they are thinking, so it is impossible to pay them back. The best thing to do when someone hurts you is to remember that what goes around comes around. If you mistreat someone, someone will mistreat you. It is a law that no human being can break. It is a bad idea to try to get even.

Well, I know what you are thinking. You are saying to yourself: "If I can't get even, what can I do when I am mistreated?" The first thing that you do is to inform the proper people. If you are mistreated in school, tell the teacher. Let someone know what has happened. Secondly, remember that you reap what you sow and it is impossible to escape when you mistreat others. Thirdly, get busy and stay busy improving yourself. The best way to get even with someone is to surpass them in every area. In other words, leave them in your dust as you get ahead in life. The best revenge is success.

Wisdom (to be discussed with your mentor)

The best manner of avenging ourselves is by not resembling him who has injured us. JANE PORTER

Revenge is biting a dog because the dog bit you.
AUSTIN O'MALLEY

Vengeance has no foresight. NAPOLEON BONAPARTE

Forgiveness is the highest and most difficult of all moral lessons. JOSEPH JACOBS

Forgiveness is man's deepest need and highest achievement. HORACE BUSHNELL

Forgiveness is the sweetest revenge.
ISAAC FRIEDMANN

The most effective recourse is the quality of your performance. Your energies should be directed to doing the best possible job you can.
CLIFTON WHARTON

Practicing the Golden Rule is not a sacrifice, it's an investment. BYLLE AVERY

Forgive, forget, and move on. DR. LOUIS SULLIVAN

Notes:_____

_____

_____

_____

_____

_____

_____

_____

_____

_____

_____

_____

_____

11. Grades! (Are They Important?)

When I was a kid, there was a time of year that I hated. It was the worst time of the year and it came four times every year. It was report card time. Back when I went to school, we were given our report cards in a brown envelope and told to take them home to our parents. This was very difficult, especially when you knew that there were some bad grades on it. There were times when I would come home late or consider joining the army to avoid showing my parents my report card. I knew they had to see it eventually because they had to sign it.

What is even more amazing is that now that I am a parent, I am very concerned with my children's report cards. Now that I am grown I realize how important grades are. Parents are concerned about their children's grades because parents have entered the work force and know from experience the importance of good grades. Parents have watched some of their friends suffer financially because they could not get good jobs. As a result of seeing what happened to their friends, parents encourage their kids to get good grades.

Our nation is filled with two types of people: skilled people and unskilled people. A skilled person is someone who has learned how to do something or has developed a skill like a doctor, nurse, engineer, teacher, or computer technician. An unskilled person sells popcorn at ball games, sweeps the floor, cuts the grass or sells hamburgers at fast food restaurants. A skilled person generally makes more money than a unskilled worker and has more benefits like hospitalization, insurance and retirement programs.

In order to become a skilled worker, there are things (skills) that you need to learn. These skills are generally learned in school, where there is a grading system. If you can't make a passing grade, you are not passed by that school and you then become classified as a unskilled worker. Please note that all honest work is good work, but usually unskilled workers work harder jobs and longer hours.

Parents want their children to have the skills that it takes to get good jobs. Parents want their children to do well long after they are dead and gone. In the United States of America you can do well if you develop the right skills. There are many ways to get skills. Before there were so many schools, young people would learn a trade from their dad or another craftsman. I have a friend whose dad was a carpenter and he helped his dad and learned a trade at the same time. He now builds houses for a living. It is always good for boys to help men who are working because you can learn many skills from them.

Good grades should be your goal, but there are some kids who work very hard and still do not make good grades. I can remember how I struggled with my multiplication tables in the third grade and my grades were not good in math. I learned that because you struggle with certain classes does not mean that you can't be successful. More importantly, you should not dislike a class just because you struggle in that class. Just because a class is difficult does not mean it can not be fun. I really enjoyed science class but it took me a few years to learn how to get a good grade out of the class.

One fact that you should keep in mind is that you are going to change a great deal in the next few years. Some subjects that are difficult now will be easier as you get older and wiser. Tell yourself that you are going to do better as time goes by. Do not turn off your hopes in the difficult subjects just because you are having a difficult time. In a few years, with some hard work, you could be the smartest kid in the class.

It is important that you learn good study habits to make sure that you are making the best possible grades that you can. There should be a place in your home where you study. Different people study best in different places. For some it is in the kitchen. Others study best in their bed room. For others it is on the living room floor. You should know where you study best and spend more time studying than you do watching television.

Never accept the idea that you can't do any better. Go to your teacher and talk to her about your grades.

Learn the grading scale, what it takes to make an excellent or "A" and what is a failing grade. Talk to the kids who make good grades and ask them how do they do it. Educating yourself about grades and the grading process will help you in your school career and will help you develop the skills you need to be successful.

Wisdom (to be read with your mentor)

You're not rewarded for having brains. You're only rewarded for using them. MORDECAI JOHNSON

If you think education is expensive—try ignorance
DEREK BOK

I have never let my schooling interfere with my education. MARK TWAIN

You don't understand anything until you learn it more than one way. MARVIN MINSKY

The best way to fight poverty is with a weapon loaded with ambition. SEPTIMA CLARK

The way to be successful is through preparation. It doesn't just happen. You don't wake up one day and discover you're a lawyer any more than you wake up as a pro football player. It takes time. ALAN PAGE

There are no shade trees on the road to success.
LEONTINE KELLY

Remember, luck is opportunity meeting up with preparation, so you must prepare yourself to be lucky. GREGORY HINES

Notes:_____

_____

_____

_____

_____

_____

_____

_____

_____

_____

_____

_____

_____

_____

12. They Made Me MAD!
(How to control your anger)

I taught elementary school for several years. It was a very exciting time in my life, and I learned many lessons from the kids that were in my classes. I can remember one day, there were two boys sitting next to each other. The boy's names were David and Jerry. David was picking on Jerry, calling him names and hitting him. As the teacher, I knew that something was going on but I could not catch them in the act. Well, David kept on picking with Jerry until Jerry snapped. At this point, Jerry jumped over the desk and began to beat David's butt. When I turned around I blamed Jerry for the disturbance, but actually he didn't start it. After I broke up the fight, I sat David and Jerry down to talk and figure out what happened.

As I talked to David and Jerry, I began to understand what had actually happened. Usually Jerry was a very good kid who never caused any problems. This is why I was surprised when I turned to see him kicking David's butt. On this occasion, Jerry had allowed his anger to get to him. Normally Jerry could ignore David when he did stupid stuff, but on this day Jerry allowed David to make him angry. As a result of getting angry, Jerry was in trouble and David almost got away without any blame.

Anger is a very interesting emotion. It can do good or it can do bad. It seems like everybody and most animals will get angry every now and then. I have seen kids, adults, dogs, cats, squirrels and even hamsters get angry. To tell the truth, I used to get angry quite often. Now that I am older, I don't get angry as much as I used to because I understand certain things about anger. Let's talk about what I have learned about anger.

1. Most of the time anger is a choice. Most of the time, we get angry because we choose to. It is a fact that *nobody* can make you angry! I have heard people say: "He or she made me angry!" That is not true. They did not make you angry. You choose to get angry.

The very, very important thing is to decide how you will respond to anger. I remember an incident that happened many years ago when I chose to get angry. Some boys were washing cars on a used car lot. Sitting beside the car lot there was a kind, gentle old man sitting down minding his own business. These mean boys took a bucket of soapy water and dumped it on the old man. When I saw this, I became very, very, very angry and chose to go talk to the car dealership and call the police. What they did to that innocent person made me mad! I responded, not by fighting but by calling the police. It is good to choose to get angry and respond when innocent people are harmed.

2. Much anger is preventable. I have decided that I will not get angry about the things that I cause because of the decisions I make. For example: At work I park my car under a tree. Every spring, the birds mess all over my car and I have to wash it almost every day. That would make me mad. Well, I have learned that if I park my car on the other side of the street, the birds will not mess on the car and I will not have anything to become angry about. Simple solutions are available for many of the things that make us angry.

What about you in your classroom or on the playground? What behavior can you change that will prevent you from becoming angry so often? I know of some boys who ask for problems by not taking preventative action. In most cases if we would do things like: stay in our seats when we're supposed to, turn homework in on time, don't talk when we shouldn't, keep our hands to ourselves, don't say mean things to other people, we would not get in trouble and we would not become angry.

On most occasions we can avoid incidents that would normally cause us to become angry. If you can't avoid the situation, stop and consider what is the proper response when you are about to get angry.

3. Respond, don't react. A reaction to anger is when you are controlled by anger. Some kids throw things, yell and hit other kids. The best thing to do when you are angry is to respond. When you respond, *you* are in control and you have the opportunity to make the right decision.

4. Most anger is not productive. Most of the time when young people get angry, they either sit around and sulk or they become aggressive. I know of students in school who become angry and pout like babies. Other students become angry and throw books, or speak in a mean tone to the teacher.

Only mature, wise people know how to make anger their friend. I am glad to say that at my age, I am pretty successful at making anger my friend. The reason I wrote this book was because I was angry. I was angry because so many boys do not have fathers and no men are spending time with them. There are other good things that I have done while angry, so I have tried to make anger my friend and not allow it to do negative things.

5. When I am angry, I don't think as clearly as I do when I am not angry. I had the opportunity to meet a man who was a 7th degree Karate black belt. This man explained to me that when he was fighting, he knew that he would beat the person if they became angry. He said: "When you get angry, I beat your butt."

The reason that he knew that he would beat you is because it is very difficult to think clearly when angry. Most boxers love to make their opponents angry because they no longer fight smart when they are angry but they begin to brawl.

Wisdom (to be discussed with your mentor)

He who conquers other is strong; He who conquers himself is mighty LAO-TZU

A soft answer turns away wrath PROVERBS 15:1

When angry, count to ten before you speak; if very angry, count to an hundred. THOMAS JEFFERSON

A angry man is again angry with himself when he returns to reason. PUBLILUS SYRUS

Anger is as a stone cast into a wasp's nest.
MALABAR PROVERB

The longer I live, the more deeply I'm convinced that the difference between the successful person and the failure, between the strong and the weak, is a decision. WILLIE E. GARY

You don't make progress by standing on the sidelines, whimpering and complaining. You make progress by implementing ideas. SHIRLEY CHISOLM

13. Trash Talkin' (Is it worth it?)

Trash talkin' is something that boys have done for years. For some boys it is considered an indoor sport. When I was a kid, we talked trash to each other all of the time. I remember on one occasion in the 4th grade, I talked trash to a kid in my homeroom named Buster. Buster was the biggest kid in the school. On this particular day he made me mad, so I talked trash to him. I told him that I was going to kick his butt and challenged him to meet me across the street from the school at 3:00. Now, I knew that I was just talking because Buster weighed about 50 pounds more than I did.

I often wondered why I would talk trash to a kid who was big enough to squash me. It was not a smart thing to do. At the end of the day when the bell rang, I got in the front of the line and I was out of the door and home before Buster caught me. Actually, I was a trash-talkin' chicken. I could not back up what I said. In some cases, boys can back up what they say, but in this case I couldn't back it up. Let's consider some reasons why boys talk trash:

1. Pride. Men and boys have a lot of pride. Pride is a overrated opinion of yourself. Because men are very prideful they have the urge to protect themselves when someone says something bad about them. Our pride is usually aroused when someone talks about us personally, talks about our mom, calls us dumb or something like that. Most of the time, when our pride is attacked we would like to fight. If we can't fight right then, we sometimes talk trash.

2. It makes us feel better. Talking trash gives us a sense of satisfaction. We feel like we have hit them with words. When kids and adults can't hit with their hands, they hit with words. Sometimes we really feel better when we hit with words and sometimes hitting with words hurts people more than hitting with hands.

3. It really hurts some kids. There are kids who don't feel good about themselves. They may not have a good home life or there may be some physical condition that they struggle with. I remember a kid in the 4th grade who could not control his bladder. He would have accidents in school and wet himself. It was not his fault; it was a medical problem. One day a mean kid talked trash to him after he had an accident and it hurt him so much that he did not come back to school for three days. Words are powerful. Words can really hurt when they are aimed at our weak spots. Everybody has weak spots, even grown men have weak spots.

4. Famous people do it. Sometimes if you watch closely, you can see basketball players talkin' trash to each other. In the movies, the stars do it all of the time. It is easy to back up what you say in the movies, but it is much harder to back up what you say on the basketball court or in real life. We need to remember that in the movies, nobody really gets hurt. In real life, trash talkin' can be very painful to the victims.

It is important to remember that your tongue is one of the smallest organs in the body but it has a power far greater than many of the other organs. The tongue can start a fire in the minds of men. Many wars have begun because of a loose tongue. Marriages have been destroyed because of loose lips. It is not good to talk all of the time. People will consider you a smart person if you just keep your mouth shut.

When you talk a lot of trash, the people around you soon know all that is in your mind and they do not consider you a very smart person. When you keep quiet, people will wonder what you are thinking and when you talk they will listen. Leave the trash talking to people who are going to live trashy lives. Decide to live with a mouth that benefits those around you.

Wisdom (to be discussed with your mentor)

The tongue is more to be feared than the sword.
JAPANESE PROVERB

I'm the son of a minister and I just can't tell dirty jokes. Even if I could, I wouldn't. You can be funny without cursing and doing sex jokes. SINBAD

If you were to make little fishes talk, they would talk like whales. OLIVER GOLDSMITH

Some things are better left not said. BERNARD SHAW

Honey, it's so easy to talk a good game. What we need are folks who will do something! MAXINE WATERS

Courage is being brave when you know something isn't going to happen to you. WILLIAM H. GRAY

Thousands of people can speak at least two languages—English and profanity. JOE CLARK

The older he grew, the less he said, and the more he spoke. BENJAMIN E. MAYS

Learn to speak kind words. Nobody resents them. CARL ROWAN

Leadership begins with sound, verbal communication skills. TERRIE WILLIAMS

Notes:_____

_____

_____

_____

_____

_____

_____

_____

_____

_____

_____

_____

_____

14. Every Boy Needs A Man In His Face

Boys are born to test the limits. Every boy will try to see how far he can go before he gets in trouble. This is a normal characteristic that boys display as they get older. I acted like this when I was a boy. The only problem that I had was that I had a father who would look at me, point his finger and tell me what was going to happen if I did the wrong thing.

I remember on one occasion that I almost smarted off to my mother. My father got in my face and said: "Son, if you smart off to your mother, I will knock your teeth out!" I knew that he was serious so I never smarted off to my mother. My father was the first man to spend some time in my face.

Another man who spent some time in my face was my first boss, Mr. Pratt. Mr. Pratt owned a music store and taught me how to work, be on time and treat customers well. I was required to be at work by four o'clock p.m. each day. Mr. Pratt would meet me at the door and shake my hand. I knew that I could not be late because Mr. Pratt would be in my face if I was late.

When I went to college I was just about grown. In spite of how old I was, I still needed a man in my face. Mr. Gillispie was the man in my face while I was in college. He taught me many things and challenged me to be my best.

The fact of the matter is that all men need an older, mature man in their face to help them do all that they should do and to be all that they can be. When you have a man in your face, several things will happen:

1. Wisdom is available to challenge you. Now that I am grown I often think of all of the stupid things that I almost did when I was younger. It was the older men that I talked to who prevented me from doing the stupid things. They challenged me with good wisdom and convinced me that what I was getting ready to do was stupid. When an older man is in your face, he is there to bring you wisdom and he is there because he cares.

2. Strength is available to control you. Every boy has what I call "wild horses" in him. Wild horses make you think that you are stronger than you are. The wild horses in you encourage you to take risks. I never will forget one day when I was in college, I decided to try to body-slam my dad who was sixty years old, but still in shape. I grabbed him from the side and was trying to lift him up when all of a sudden the world began to spin. Dad had somehow managed to pick me up, spin me around and throw me down. Even though he was older, he was still able to control me.

Young boys need to realize that there are men who are stronger than they are. They are able to control you if they need to. This is good and not bad because most boys go through periods in their lives where they need help managing their wild horses.

3. Wisdom and strength are available to cover your back. In this life there are many things that you cannot control, things that are behind your back and you cannot see them. There are other things that you are not wise enough to see that an older man is aware of. A man in your face can warn you of the things that are behind your back and can alert you to the dangers that you can't see.

When we make mistakes in life, we need wisdom and strength to help us to recover and get our feet back on the ground. A man in your face will provide that for you. The idea of having a man in your face will work to make you a better man when you get older. I often think of the men who were in my face while I was forming my personality. Young men are in the process of forming their personalities and lives. A man in your face will guide the process and help you reach your full potential in the years to come. The only thing that society has to make men out of is boys. A man in a boy's face is a great gift to the boy and the community. I challenge you to get some men in your face so that you can be the best that you can be.

Wisdom (to be discussed with your mentor)

A good example is the best sermon. THOMAS FULLER

Don't ask for anyone's advice unless you are prepared to use it. SAMMY DAVIS

A person isn't educated unless he has learned how little he already knows. THOMAS A. FLEMING

Children could keep on the straight and narrow path if they could get information from someone who's been over the route. MARIAN WRIGHT EDLEMAN

It embarrasses me to think of all those years I was buying silk suits and alligator shoes that were hurting my feet; cars that I just parked, and the dust would just build up on them. GEORGE FOREMAN

A person is never what he ought to be until he is doing what he ought to be doing. BUSTER SOARIES

The wounds of a friend are better than the kisses of an enemy. PROVERBS 27:6

15. My Teacher, My Friend

My favorite teacher in middle school was Mrs. Thompson. I can remember her today just as if I was still in her 7th grade science class. I have often tried to figure out why I liked Mrs. Thompson so much. I believe that one reason I liked her was that I knew that she wanted what was best for me. I knew that when she fussed at me, it was because she wanted me to do my best.

To tell the truth, there were many days when I did not do my best, and she would fuss at me. I think it is important to know the difference between when a teacher gets on you because she wants you to do better and when she gets on you because she is having a bad day. Mrs. Thompson would get on me because she cared for me and she would not accept second best.

A good teacher is like a gold mine that you need to dig in to get all of the riches out of your relationship with her. Teachers have the ability to look at kids and see abilities and strengths that may one day make them great. When a teacher tells you that you can do better, she generally does it for two reasons:

1. She feels that you really can do better. When my teacher made me do a project over it was because she wanted me to do my best. When I was young I thought that she wanted me to do it over because she

77

was mean. When teachers don't like you, they let you do badly and don't care about it. When teachers like you very much, they insist that you do your best and they may bug you until you do the work correctly.

2. She wants to encourage you to do better. Young people don't realize the benefits of doing your best. Many kids just want to do enough to get by. When you do this, you are cheating yourself. A good teacher will try to help you see that you can do better and encourage you to do better. If your teacher is that kind of teacher, then she is a good teacher.

One of the problems with being a kid is that you do not understand the future. Teachers understand the future because they are older than you are. When a teacher looks at you and says that you are not doing your best, she is usually thinking about your future. She knows that time is moving on and that if you don't do your best you will be behind and have a hard time catching up.

It really hurts elementary school teachers when they hear that students that they had are now in high school and are not doing well or dropping out. As a matter of fact, teachers often feel a sense of personal failure when their students don't do well. Teachers also know that no matter how hard they work, success in the classroom is ultimately up to the student. A teacher is not your mother or father, but a person who comes along to help your parents give you an education. Let me give you some suggestions on how to really benefit from the time you spend with your teacher:

1. Always cooperate fully with your teacher. It is a fact that you are the student and he/she is the teacher. There will be times when you do not understand what he/she is doing or why she is doing it. If you understood it all, you would be the teacher.

2. Be honest with your teacher and tell him/her when and where you are struggling with particular subjects. The worst thing that you can do is to pretend that everything is all right when it isn't. If you don't ask for help when you need it, you are not helping your teacher to help you. Learn to look your teacher in the eye and say: "I need some help with this subject." Not only will it help you in that particular subject, but it will also help you as you relate to adults.

3. Use the best manners that you know. Saying things like: "Yes, Miss Johnson," and "No, Miss Johnson," will most definitely help your relationship. It is a funny thing, but adults will generally go out of their way to help a kid who has good manners.

4. Remember that your teacher is a person too. She may have kids and problems of her own. If she makes an occasional mistake, don't be surprised, but allow her to be human just like you are. There are days when teachers are low on energy and need to take it slow. Be helpful on days like this and don't make his/her day worse.

What can you do today to help your teacher have a better day? I want to challenge you to be the student in your class who keeps a good attitude toward your teacher. Regardless of what the other kids do, you should be the one who shows your teacher appreciation by keeping a good attitude.

Wisdom (to be discussed with your mentor)

A teacher affects eternity; he/she can never tell where his influence stops. HENRY ADAMS

Each friend represents a world in us, a world possibly not born until they arrive, and it is only by this meeting that a new world is born. ANAIS NIN

Teachers, who educate children, deserve more honor than parents, who merely gave them birth; for the latter provided mere life, while the former ensure a good life. ARISTOTLE

You shall judge a man by his foes as well as by his friends. JOSEPH CONRAD

Chance makes our parents, but choice makes our friends. JACQUES DELILLE

A teacher is the child's third parent. HYMAN MAXEWLL
BERSTON

*The friend is the man/woman who knows all about
you, and still likes you.* ELBERT HUBBARD

*Perhaps the most valuable result of all education is
the ability to make yourself do the thing you have to
do, when it ought to be done, whether you like it or
not.* WALTER BAGEHOT

A hand up is better than a hand out. SYBIL MOBLEY

Notes:_____

_____

_____

_____

_____

_____

_____

_____

16. TV And Reality

I am so old that I can remember when television was still new. At that time, only a few people in the neighborhood had televisions. I remember when the day came when we finally got one at our house. Back then, everything on television was good and there was no need for ratings or for your parents to tell you not to watch certain programs. Today, young people need to be careful what they watch because there are some programs that are only for adults and are about things that may be too stressful for young people. Things like violence, sex, and other shows that teach young people things that they should not learn until they are 17 years old or older.

There are some young people who have a problem telling the difference between fantasy and reality. For example, one of my favorite shows when I was a kid was The Three Stooges. They would do all sorts of things like falling down stairs, hitting each other on the head with hammers and stuff like that. The interesting thing is that they never got hurt. Well, my friend Dugan tried to do one of the tricks that we watched the Three Stooges do on TV. The trick didn't work and Dugan ended up in the hospital with three stitches in his forehead. His mom was mad! She said that we could not watch television for a whole month.

Television is not all bad, but you must learn to watch it with your brain really alert to tell the difference between what is real and what is not real. I love to watch TV and see if I can see what is real and what is not real. I can remember watching one episode of *Gun Smoke* when Matt Dillon, who was the Sheriff in Dodge City, got into a fight with a bad guy. They rolled around in the dirt, punching, kicking and choking each other for about two minutes. The amazing thing was that when Matt Dillon got up, his shirt was clean. So, I realized that Matt Dillon was not rolling around in the dirt but that it was a stunt man. I still enjoy watching movies today to find mistakes like this.

Today, I believe that we need to look for flawed messages when we watch TV and movies. There are many messages given through TV shows that you really need to think about. For example, I watched a show about a man who was running from the law. This man very successfully escaped from the law several times. Each time he escaped, he made the police look very foolish. Now, this is fantasy because I know some policemen who are ten times smarter than the policemen in the TV show and they would have caught him the first time they tried.

We must be careful to look at things realistically rather than believing everything that we see on TV. Today we have a lot of copycats who imitate anything that they see on TV. Guns on TV don't hurt anybody because they use blanks. In real life, guns kill you and should be avoided at all costs. On TV they punch you in the stomach five times, kick you in the head eight times, and stomp on you four times, and you still get up and fight some more. In real life, one kick to the head can kill you.

One of the joys of being young is that you are impressionable. In other words, you believe much of what you hear and see. The problem with being young and impressionable is that you don't have the discernment to know what is real and what is fantasy. Discernment is the ability to tell something real from something not real. The older you get, the more discernment that you have. This is why it is so important to ask an adult about the TV shows that you watch. Adults know that you don't have as much discernment as you will have in a few years. This why they don't want you to watch certain shows.

When I was a kid, I was afraid of the monster shows. And yet, I would stay up late Saturday night and watch *The Monster Who Ate Up New York*. The problem was that after watching the show, I could not go to sleep. I did not have the ability to discern between TV and reality. I felt that the monster that ate up New York would soon eat up my house, so I stayed up all night.

It is important that we guard our minds and protect them from things that would affect us in a bad way.

Violence, sexual activity, profanity, and other bad things should not be seen by young people because the images will stick in your mind and affect you negatively. Television is a wonderful invention that can be used for good or for bad. If you choose to watch all shows with discernment, turning off the bad shows, you will use television for good. When you do this, you will control the television and it will not control you.

Wisdom (to be discussed with your mentor)

Human kind cannot bear very much reality.

T.S. ELIOT

All television is educational television. The question is: what is it teaching? NICHOLAS JOHNSON

Everything is a dangerous drug except reality, which is unendurable. CYRIL CONNOLLY

Facts are facts and will not disappear on account of your likes. JAWAHARLAL NHRU

Living in Hollywood can give you a false sense of reality. I try to stay in touch with my inner feelings–that's what's really going on. WILL SMITH

Thoughts have power; thoughts are energy. And you can make your world or break it by your own thinking. SUSAN TAYLOR

No life will ever be great until it is dedicated and disciplined. PETER C. B. BYNOE

Television is an invention that permits you to be entertained in your living room by people you wouldn't have in your home. DAVID FROST

Of all the dramatic media, radio is the most visual.
JOHN REEVES

Notes:_____

_____

_____

_____

_____

_____

_____

_____

_____

_____

_____

_____

_____

_____

_____

17. Family Equals Joy And Pain

I am the son of a man who had ten children. These people are called my family. There are days when I am very glad that I have them as my family, and there are other days when I wish that they were not born. Take my younger brother David (names have been changed to protect the guilty) for example. He is a great guy. If you met him, you would want him to be your friend. The only problem is that he has a drug problem that he can't control. So, on one hand, I love to be around him and I love him, but on the other hand, he hurts my heart because of what he does. Family equals joy and pain.

I know many young people who have family members whom they love very much. Unfortunately, some of their bad habits or actions also cause pain. When you are young you often feel helpless to change some of the pain that you are feeling about your family. What I find interesting is that even when you grow up, there will still be pain and disappointment that you will have to learn to live with. It takes years to learn how to live with a family that brings joy one day and pain the next day. I have learned some things about families that I want to share with you.

1. We love family members even if we don't love what they do. A human being is the most valuable thing on this planet. It is very important that we learn at an early age to love people even if we hate what they do. I love my brother David but I hate what he does. What he does brings me pain, but he brings me joy. Remember that family members deserve and need your love, even when they do not behave as they should.

2. You can't change the way anybody acts. No human being can change the behavior of another human being. Children often plead, pray, and beg for their parents and other loved ones to behave a certain way. Many times young people will feel very guilty about the behavior of other family members. Some kids even feel that it is their fault when their parents divorce. This is not true! No human being is responsible for the behavior of another, and you can not change the way another person acts.

3. Learn to separate yourself from their bad behavior. I can remember that one day I gave David a ride in my car. What I did not know was that David had a rock of cocaine in his pocket. We were not stopped by the police or anything, but if we had been stopped, I would have gone to jail because of my brother. What I learned to do was to be careful how and when I would hang out with David. People who have unacceptable behaviors can get you into trouble if you are not careful. It is possible to start doing what they do if you don't pay attention. Bad company corrupts good habits. Don't be afraid to tell them "I am not going to do that with you or hang with you while you do that."

4. Always leave the door of hope open because they might change. I have a friend who was an alcoholic for many years. One day he decided that he was not going to take another drink. Believe it or not, it has been nine years and he has not had another drink. Friends and family members must always believe that change is possible. You may even want to encourage them by telling them that you believe that they can change and maybe one day it will happen.

Because families are central to our lives, we need to learn how to deal with the ups and downs they bring to our lives. Every family has its ups and downs, and when you get married and have children there will be good days and bad days. The only thing that we can do is to continue to love our families. We must remember that we cannot make them act a certain way. We also must determine that we will not copy their negative behavior.

Wisdom (to be discussed with your mentor)

I don't know who my grandfather was; I am much more concerned to know what his grandson will be.
ABRAHAM LINCOLN

To the family—that dear octopus from whose tentacles we never quite escape, nor in our inmost hearts, ever quite wish to. DODIE SMITH

The proper time to influence the character of a child is about 100 years before he is born. DEAN WILLIAM R. INGE

Find the good and praise it. ALEX HALEY

From the day you're born until the day you ride in a hearse, there's nothing so bad that it couldn't be worse. SMOKEY ROBINSON

My mother told me I was capable of doing anything. "Be ambitious," she said. "Jump at de sun." ZORA NEALE HURSTON

I'm not a self-made man. I cannot forget those who have sacrificed for me to get where I am today. JESSIE HILL

The most lonely place in the world is the human heart when love is absent. SADIE ALEXANDER

Everything in the household runs smoothly when love oils the machinery. WILLIAM H. GRIER

Notes:_____

_____

_____

_____

_____

_____

_____

_____

_____

_____

_____

_____

_____

_____

_____

18. Girls (Sugar And Spice And Everything Nice)

Girls are special. Wait a minute, wait a minute! Let me explain what I mean. If you were to talk to a grown man, most of them would tell you that some of the most exciting times that they have had in life is the time they have spent with girls. Now, when you are in the fourth grade, you don't know very much about girls and you are not supposed to. As boys get older, they begin to take an interest in girls and really start studying them.

It takes most boys a long time to understand girls. Most husbands work hard to understand why their wives do what they do. I really think this is great because it keeps us interested in them. Girls would be boring if we completely understood them all the time.

One of these days you will be interested in girls and when you grow up you may get married and live with a woman every day. There are some important facts that every boy should know about girls. These facts will help as you relate to all females; including mother, teacher, and future girlfriend.

1. Treat them with kindness and respect. Girls love to be treated kindly. As a matter of fact, most human beings like to be treated that way, but I think that girls really appreciate being treated that way.

2. Give them sincere compliments. We all like to be complimented. Be sure to always compliment girls on who they are and not only on how they look. Please notice that I said: "sincere compliments." Don't overdo it.

3. Treat them like you would want a man to treat your mother. There is a principle that you cannot escape which says whatever you dish out to others will eventually come back to you. If you have seen women being abused in any way, you must determine that you will not do that. You have the privilege of starting a new way of doing things when you get a girlfriend. Always think about your mother when you deal with girls.

4. Never, as long as your heart is beating, hit a woman! Any man who would hit a woman is a low-down dirty dog. I can hear someone asking the question: "What if she hits me first?" Well, if she hits you first you have several options: 1. Walk away. 2. Tell an adult. 3. If possible, reason with her and tell that you do not like to be hit upon. In most cases you can avoid hitting her back if you use your head.

5. Learn to become a servant to women and you will find that all of your needs will be met. When you get older and enter into a relationship, what you are actually agreeing to do is to serve the other person. Marriage is a commitment to serve the person that you are married to. All relationships with women prior to marriage are warm-ups for the real thing. In other words, if you want a good relationship, you must learn to develop the mindset of a servant.

Now, let me hurry up and say that this applies to the woman too. In a relationship she will be your servant also. So each person is serving the other person's needs.

Wisdom (to be discussed with your mentor)

A woman is the only thing I am afraid of that I know will not hurt me. ABRAHAM LINCOLN

Treat the older women as mothers, and the girls as your sisters, thinking only pure thoughts about them. PAUL OF TARSHISH

A woman is like a tea bag—only in hot water do you realize how strong she is. NANCY REAGAN

A woman's strength is the irresistible might of weakness. RALPH WALDO EMERSON

Women who set a low value on themselves make life hard for all women. NELLIE McCLUNG

A homely girl hates mirrors. PROVERB

A girl is Innocence playing in the mud, Beauty standing on its head, and Motherhood dragging a doll by the foot. ALLAN BECK

Don't be upset if your dreams don't come true. It could be the best thing that ever happened to you. SHARI BELAFONTE

Notes:_____

_____

_____

_____

_____

_____

_____

_____

_____

_____

_____

_____

_____

_____

_____

19. I Got Busted, And I Didn't Do It!

I will never forget that Tuesday morning after recess when all the boys were allowed to go to the bathroom. We had been outside playing, and the teacher told us to come in. We were told to go to the bathroom before we went back to our classroom. While in the bathroom, a very interesting thing happened. My friend Richard and a few other guys started making a lot of noise, screaming, banging on the paper towel dispenser and other things. Now, everybody was making some noise. but only a few guys were making most of the noise.

When we came out of the bathroom, Miss McFever was very angry. She started fussing at everybody when Richard, my supposed friend, turned around, looked at me and said: "He was banging on the paper towel dispenser." Now, I was in shock because that was a "bold face *lie*!" I didn't think that the teacher would believe him, but she did. Now, you won't believe what happened next. The teacher took me, only me, to the side and sent the rest of the class to the room. She then took one of those little paddles you bounce the ball on and gave me five swats on my butt. That hurt really bad. Now, I want to tell you the truth. I wanted to KILL Richard!, I wanted to KILL Richard!, I wanted to rip his brains out with my bare hands!

We all know that it is illegal to kill people even though they are the cause of you getting "The Paddle." Now, I want you to put yourself in my shoes:

1. Your butt is throbbing!
2. You hate Richard and want to kill him!
3. You are not guilty but nobody believes you!

These are days when you wish you had stayed in bed. These are days when you really need to think as you try to figure out what to do. It is very hard to think when you have been lied about and you are forced to suffer unjustly, but if you want to succeed in life, you need to learn how to do it.

It takes great wisdom to keep your mouth shut when you are busted for no reason. Sometimes it is better to let things cool down and then go to the teacher and ask her if you could speak to her for a minute. If you give situations time they will often work themselves out. I know of a situation where a girl lied, lied, lied all of the time and got people in trouble. The only problem was she looked like a little angel and the teacher always believed her. One day when she wasn't paying attention, the teacher was standing behind her and the teacher heard her using profanity and lying. From that day on, whenever she told the teacher something, the teacher would really check out what she was saying.

Whenever you get caught up in a negative situation where there is a lot of confusion, cool out. Let the dust settle and then try to talk it out. If it happens that you are busted and you didn't do it, no big deal. The person who got you in trouble will have their turn. What goes around, comes around.

I often thought about getting even with stupid Richard. What if I had thrown my history book at him while sitting behind him in class, or, sliced the tires on his bicycle, or got even in some very creative way? In reality, the guy who hits back always gets caught. In basketball, the referee will often miss a foul, but he always sees it when the guy hits back.

Wise men learn how to overlook minor offenses. In other words, wise men don't seek to get even for every little wrong that they suffer because if you do, it will only get you into further trouble. What about you? If you were me and Richard got you busted, what would you do?

Wisdom (to be discussed with your mentor)

It is a smaller thing to suffer punishment than to have deserved it. OVID

The innocent is the person who explains nothing. ALBERT CAMUS

Whosoever blushes is already guilty; true innocence is ashamed of nothing. HENRY DAVID THOREAU

In law a man is guilty when he violates the rights of another. In ethics he is guilty if he only thinks of doing so. IMMANUEL KANT

Even doubtful accusations leave a stain behind them. THOMAS FULLER

Character is what you have left when you've lost everything else. PATRICIA HARRIS

There is more power in the open hand than in the clenched fist. MARTIN LUTHER KING JR.

One of the highest forms of human maturity is taking full responsibility for what happens to you.

B.J. TATUM

Notes:_____

_____

_____

_____

_____

_____

_____

_____

_____

_____

_____

_____

_____

_____

20. Stupid Stuff

One of the problems of being a boy is that boys sometimes do stupid stuff. Girls often tell us that we do stupid stuff and we blow them off and try to ignore them. The fact of the matter is, boys do stupid stuff. As a grown man, I often look back to when I was a child and I remember the stupid stuff that I used to do. I can remember that I would operate on all of my sisters dolls and take the little motors out of them. Not only was this stupid, but it was mean. My sister would pick her dolls up and try to get them to move, but she did not know that I had taken the motors out of them.

I can remember riding my bicycle off the top of the hill at full speed, getting up to about 40 miles per hour without a helmet on. That's just plain stupid! Some of my friends did some really stupid stuff. I can remember them trying to talk me into doing some stupid stuff with them. Sometimes I did and sometimes I didn't. One time, they put a long board up to the side of the school and they climbed up the board and got on the roof. They challenged me to climb up too. They were all older than I was and much bigger. I remember struggling to climb up the board like the big boys. When I finally got on the top of the roof, the big boys jumped off and took the board down. I had to stay up on the roof until my father came and got me. Now, that was stupid!

I have often tried to think of the reasons why people do stupid things. I have come up with some reasons:

1. To get attention. It is a fact that everybody needs attention. The problem is that some people don't know how to get it without acting stupid. They act stupid hoping that others will look at them. When people look at them, they feel better about themselves because they are getting the attention that they desire.

2. Because they don't know any better. Some people don't have what I call "Good Home Training." Good home training is where your parents teach you basic social skills like not to pick your nose in public, to open the door for elderly people, to say "Yes sir" and "Yes ma'am, "Yes, Mr. Johnson" or "No Mr. Johnson." We have many young people today who have not been taught basic social skills, and they don't know any better than to act up in public to get attention.

3. They don't understand the consequences. I have a friend who was very stupid when he was younger. He told me that he and some of his friends did some wrong things and got caught. When they stood before the judge, they were arrogant (thought they were badd). They told the judge to go ahead and give them time, they could do whatever he dished out. Well, the judge gave them all one year in the penitentiary. They turned and walked out of the courtroom like they were badd. What is interesting is that once they got in prison, my friend said that he and all of his buddies cried every day and every night. They realized that they did not understand what prison was like and that they were stupid when they acted the way they acted.

4. They hang around with stupid friends. It is a fact that all people eventually act like those they hang out with. The reason why so many young people do drugs is because they hang out in a drug- infested environment. It is a fact of human behavior that you act like the people you hang out with. In the next chapter we'll talk more about this.

I am so excited that as a man I do not do as many stupid things now as I did when I was a boy, but men occasionally do stupid things. As I get older and wiser, I am learning how to leave the stupid things to stupid people, and I am trying to live a wise life and do wise things. What about you?

Wisdom (to be discussed with your mentor)

It's like this: When I was a child I spoke and thought and reasoned as a child does. But when I became a man my thoughts grew far beyond those of my childhood, and now I have put away the childish things. I CORINTHIANS 13:11

A fool always finds a bigger fool to admire him. NICOLAS BOILEAU

Common sense is very uncommon. HORACE GREELEY

Lost time is never found again. THELONIOUS MONK

It is better to look where you are going than to see where you have been. FLORENCE GRIFFITH-JOYNER

The difference between genius and stupidity is that genius has its limits. ANONYMOUS

Stupidity is an elemental force for which no earthquake is a match. KARL KRAUS

Never underestimate the power of stupid people in large groups. ANONYMOUS

Stupidity is the night of the mind, but a night without moon or star. CONFUCIUS

21. Who Do You Act Like?

I am amazed at how many children act just like their parents act. When you live with people, you unconsciously begin to talk like them and pick up many of their behaviors. These behaviors may be negative or they may be positive. As I get older, I find that I have many of my dad's good and bad habits. I really did not realize that I acted so much like him, but my wife and my mother are always noticing many of his characteristics in my behavior.

We are all prisoners of our environment. We pick up words, movements, and mannerisms from those around us. Stop and think for a moment about the words that the kids in your class use. How many words have you learned from them this year? What is the latest slang word that has hit your class or school? We all are influenced by our environment, whether negative or positive, and we all act like somebody.

The million dollar question is: "Who do you act like?" Do you really know the person who most influences you? Do you know why you act like that person? Have you thought about whether you should act like this person? As a parent, I am very careful about the TV shows and movies that I allow my children to watch. I have learned that my kids start to act like whoever they see on TV. Not too long ago, I purchased a video for my kids to watch, and

111

they learned all of the words on the video. They watched it over and over and over again. Soon they had almost memorized the whole video.

We must remember that we all learn about life by watching others. This can be a really good habit if we are watching the right people. Let me ask you a question: When it comes to study habits, who is the best person in your class to watch? When it comes to good manners and politeness, who is the best person in your class to watch? When you go outside to play ball, who has the best talent out there?

My advice to you is to find people who are good at doing the right thing and then watch them and imitate them. There is nothing wrong with giving them a compliment and letting them know that you admire them in that area. No person has it together in every area, but we all have something that we do well and others can learn from us. Who do you act like? Well, for me, I act like different people in different things.

When it comes to being a good father, I act like my dad. When it comes to cooking, I act like my mother. When it comes to teaching, I act like Mr. Jenkins, my favorite junior high school teacher. It is good to know who you copied all of your good habits from.

When my daughter was in kindergarten, we learned that we could not allow her to hear any bad language because she would repeat it. One day she stayed with a friend who was watching an adult-rated movie. This friend did not think that my daughter would pay any attention to the movie, but she came home saying some of the bad things that were in the movie. It was easy for us to tell where she learned the words because she had not been anyplace else.

Discovering why you act the way you act is a great accomplishment. Once you discover why you act the way you act, you can change the things you want to change. I want to challenge you to take the time to think about your family and some of the behaviors that you see in your home. Every home has some good behaviors and some bad behaviors. We should always try to imitate the good behaviors of our parents and not imitate their bad behaviors.

My mother was a wonderful mother for us kids. She had many good behaviors that I tried to imitate. She also had one bad habit that I did not want to imitate, and that was cigarettes. Back then, it was cool to smoke and everybody did it but it just didn't seem right to me. I am glad that I did not act like my mother in that area. Well, your life will be modeled after someone that you are around. It is up to you to choose who you want to act like. You can control your behavior by making a decision not to imitate the way certain people act. When you make these decisions every day, you are taking control of your life. Good luck as you decide who you want to act like.

Wisdom (to be discussed with your mentor)

If I try to be like him, who will be like me?
YIDDISH PROVERB

We love in others what we lack in ourselves, and would be everything but what we are. R. H. STODDARD

When people are free to do as they please, they usually imitate each other. ERIC HOFFER

Nothing is so soothing to our self-esteem as to find our bad traits in our forebears. It seems to absolve us. VAN WYCK BROOKS

The question is not always where we stand but in which direction we are headed. MARY FRANCES BERRY

To do exactly the opposite is also a form of imitation. GEORG C. LICHTENBERG

A man becomes like those whose society he loves.
HINDU PROVERB

22. Moral Restraints
(What are they, and who needs them?)

Not too long ago I heard of a terrible, terrible situation where two boys, both in elementary school contributed to the death of another boy their age. Actually, what they did was they killed him and they did it like it was a game. I asked myself how these young boys could do such a dastardly deed and make a joke out of it. The truth is that there are some things that are morally wrong and others things that are morally right. Unfortunately, there are those in our society who either don't know the difference or don't care.

Some people in our society do not have what is called moral restraints. In other words, there is no little voice in their head telling them what is right or wrong. They do whatever they want to do, regardless of how it will affect themselves or other people. Another way to say this is that some people do not have a conscience. Our conscience is our moral warning system that goes off when we do something wrong. When you do wrong, your conscience will make you feel guilty even if you never get caught by an adult.

I can still remember the day that I did something really bad. I played a trick on Terry Wayne. There was a hornet's nest in a path behind our house. I told Terry Wayne to race me to the other side of the field, knowing that he would have to run through the hornet's nest. I knew that what I was doing was wrong, but I did not use restraint. In other words, I did it anyway. Well, we raced and Terry Wayne was stung very badly by three bees. I can remember looking in his back door watching his mother pull the stingers out of his head. At first it was funny, but later I really felt bad about what I had done. My conscience was bothering me.

I am glad that I had a conscience when I was a kid. My conscience kept me out of a lot of trouble. On many occasions I would listen to that little voice that would say: "Don't do that" when I was about to do something wrong. I have learned that if you listen to that little voice before you do wrong, it will be a little voice that warns you. If you don't listen before you do wrong, that little voice will become a big voice that will bug you after you do wrong.

Moral restraints are needed to keep our society healthy. If everybody decided that they were going to do what they wanted to and ignore moral restraints, our society would collapse. The bad things that you see happening to other countries on television would soon occur in our cities here in the United States of America.

If there were no moral restraints in our society, people would raid the malls and take what they wanted. They would kill you or me for no reason at all. Robbery, rape, beatings and burnings would be happening all around us. Life as we know it would soon end.

We cannot afford to allow this to happen to our country. The only way to stop it is for people to impose moral restraints on themselves. For example, I do not allow myself to steal. I don't mess around with other men's wives. I vote for laws that will help men and women with their moral restraints. I vote against laws that would encourage people to do wrong.

History tells us that the greatest nations that ever existed were not destroyed by invading armies that came from far away. Instead, they were destroyed by their own citizens when almost everybody in the country refused to have moral restraints and did what they wanted to do even when it was wrong. The ancient empire of Rome is the best example of a nation that destroyed itself. Take time to look it up in the encyclopedia and see for yourself.

Having a good system of moral restraints will help you in all of your endeavors. You develop your moral restraints from your early training when you are told to respect other people and treat them like you would like to be treated. Decide now to be a moral leader in your school, community and country. America needs more young men like you to keep it the great nation that it is. If you don't do it, it won't be done.

Wisdom (to be discussed with your mentor)

What you ought to do, you should do; and what you should do, you ought to do. OPRAH WINFREY

Of all the qualities necessary for success, none comes before character. ERNESTA PROCOPE

The collapse of character begins with compromise.
FREDERICK DOUGLASS

Not to have control over the senses is like sailing in a rudderless ship, bound to break to pieces on coming in contact with the very first rock.
MAHATMA GANDHI

Moral restraint is feeling temptation and resisting it.
SIGMUND FREUD

Moral restraint is drawing the line somewhere.
GILBERT KEITH CHESTERTON

Moral courage is a more rare commodity than bravery in battle or great intelligence.
ROBERT F. KENNEDY

You've got to be brave and you've got to be bold. Brave enough to take your chance on your own discrimination--what's right and what's wrong, what's good and what's bad. ROBERT FROST

23. How to Change Your Bad Habits

When I think of my elementary school days, I think of a period in my life when it seemed like I was trying to do what everybody told me to do. My mother always had a list of things for me to do. So did my dad. If you add to that my teachers, aunties, and older brothers and sisters, I know that you will see what I mean. It seemed like everybody was my boss. So, the way I dealt with that situation was this: I rebelled. In other words when my mother told me to pick up my clothes, I would try to see how long I could let them stay on the floor. I developed an attitude of trying to do things my way, regardless of how illogical it was.

When young people do this, they will eventually develop some bad habits. Needless to say, here I am, a grown man and I am still trying to get rid of some of the bad habits that I developed when I was in the fifth grade. One habit I am working on is to make sure that all of my clothes are hung up as soon as I take them off. When my mother told me to do this, I felt that she was nagging, but now that I am married, my wife says the same things that my mother did.

What I have come to realize is that if you have a bad habit, you will never be able to outlive or outrun it. The only hope is to overcome it. So, here I am, a grown man, still working hard to make sure that my clothes are hung up at the end of the day. I guess there are some things that we naturally rebel against. I have a friend who just won't stop smoking. He started when he was younger and he knows that it is bad, but he just won't stop. I have another friend who has a bad habit of reading while he drives. Even though he has had one accident, he still won't work to break that bad habit.

Well, enough about me and my friends. What about you and your friends? We need to remember that bad habits do several negative things:

1. They affect others. If you smoke, drink, do hard drugs, lie, steal or cheat, your bad habit hurts other people. I know a man who steals to support his drug habit and he told me that he didn't hurt anyone. The fact of the matter is that even though you may not hurt people directly, you can hurt people indirectly. For example, if you smoke it hurts you directly but it hurts others indirectly when you get sick and others must take care of you.

2. They slow us down. Just take my bad habit (that I used to have) of not hanging up my clothes. This habit cost me time and money because when you don't hang up your clothes you will have a disorganized room and it will take you longer to get going in the morning. Also, your clothes get dirty and wrinkled faster.

3. They cause us to get lower grades. Can you remember the old excuse: "The dog ate my homework?" This is the excuse of a person who was not organized, which is a bad habit. Your bad habits will contribute to low grades. For example, if you don't have a place in your home where you do your homework, you are disorganized. You should find a spot that your family will agree to be your homework spot. It may be the kitchen table, the living room floor or your bedroom, but you need a spot where you can get in the habit of working.

People who get ahead in life are those who are never happy with second best. If you have bad habits that you can change, that is second best. Let me tell you what to do if you want to change a bad habit.

1. Talk to yourself and tell yourself that you can change. Convincing yourself is a very important place to start. If you don't believe that you can change, you never will change. When there is no one to encourage you, talk to yourself. I have learned to talk to myself when I am discouraged or weak. I tell myself that I can do it.

2. Find a friend who will encourage you. If you have another person in your life who wants to see you do better and will encourage you, that will help. I have a friend who is very neat. There are times when he makes me sick, but most of the time he encourages me to do better with my neatness and I encourage him to stop reading while he drives.

3. With a very stubborn attitude, start practicing the behavior that you desire. For me, it was picking up my clothes no matter how lousy it made me feel, no matter how big a rush I was in or if my brother had stolen all of my hangers.

4. Continue practicing the new behavior until it becomes natural. Believe it or not, any behavior that you repeat often enough will eventually become natural. You can do anything over and over and over and it will become a habit. The first thing that I think of is the first time I saw someone smoke their first cigarette. After the first puff, they cough and choke a few times. After a few days, they can suck smoke into their lungs and never cough. The reason this happens is because the human body adjusts to the intrusion of the smoke into the lungs and will even begin to demand cigarettes on a regular basis.

This is the same thing that happens when we begin to change our habits. Believe it or not, if you were to come to my bedroom you would not find any clothes on the floor. They would all be hanging up. Did this happen overnight? No way! It took some time while I practiced appropriate behavior.

I have a background in music and I can say from experience that when a person begins to play an instrument that it will be awkward and difficult to play a scale but after a little practice it can be done with ease. This is how you can overcome your bad habits and help others overcome theirs.

5. If you are not working on your bad habits, you are not growing. Some people never grow in life because they never challenge their bad habits. If you are challenging your bad habits, then you will someday soon be a mature adult who has it together. Good luck as you tackle those bad habits that are in your life. Remember, be sure to celebrate every time you overcome one.

Wisdom (to be discussed with your mentor)

A habit is something you can do without thinking-- which is why most of us have so many of them.
FRANKLIN CLARK

Habit is the test of truth: It must be right, I've done it from my youth. GEORGE CRABBE

Habits are chains too small to be felt till they are too strong to be broken. SAMUEL JOHNSON

Excellence is to do a common thing in an uncommon way. BOOKER T. WASHINGTON

It's no disgrace to start over or to begin anew.
BEBE MOORE CAMPBELL

I've always believed no matter how many shots I miss, I'm going to make the next one. ISAIAH THOMAS

It's not a question of can you succeed; a better question is will you succeed. GEORGE JOHNSON

The person who is self-centered is off-centered. SIMON ESTES

Responsibility develops some individuals and ruins others. ROBERT WOODSON

The secret to getting things done is to act! BENJAMIN O. DAVID

Notes:_____

_____

_____

_____

_____

_____

_____

_____

_____

_____

_____

_____

_____

_____

24. Peach People
(Understanding Different Races)

I really enjoy being around little kids because they are a lot of fun. One of the joys of being a parent is that kids bring a feeling of innocence to your world. Little children believe in kindness, gentleness, sharing and good stuff like that. Unless an older person teaches them to, they do not hate anybody.

When my first child was little, she went to a preschool where for the first time, she met kids who were different than she was. Some of these kids had skin of a different color and different hair. My daughter found this very interesting but not threatening. I will never forget the day that I picked her up from pre-school and she told me about her day. She said: "Daddy, I made a new friend today." I said: "You did? What is your new friend's name?" She said: "My friend's name is Jennifer, she is one of the Peach People." I said: "Peach People?" She said: "Yes, Peach People."

I was puzzled, trying to understand what this 5-year-old meant by "Peach people." I had never heard of Peach People. Well, she went on to explain that Peach People had straight hair and skin that looked like a peach. I finally understood what she was talking about. She was talking about "White" or Caucasian people.

What I found interesting was that this 5-year-old did not know that they were called "White people" so she made up her own name and called them Peach People. This innocent child did not understand anything about different races. All she knew was that she had a new friend whose skin reminded her of a peach, so she called her a Peach Person. I think it is great when a child innocently makes up a name for people of different races. It is terrible when kids learn bad names about other races from mean adults.

We live in the United States of America, a great nation that has been built by many different races. Regardless of what race you may be, we all need to learn to be like the 5-year-old who sees all people as possible friends regardless of the color of their skin.

As an adult, I have learned to pick my friends because of how nice they are and not by the color of their skin. All races have nice people and all races have mean people. I want to have nice people as my friends, regardless of their race. There is a lot we can learn as we spend time with people who are different than we are. I am not saying that everybody has to be your friend but I am saying that you should not prejudge a person because of how they look.

We must also be careful about the words we use when those who are different are not around. What language do you use in your home to describe different races of people? Do you use words that others would approve of? What we say about people behind their back is a good indicator of how we really feel about them. This is why it is very important to be careful about the words we use to describe others.

People who choose not to interact with people of a different race are missing opportunities for growth that will help them get ahead in life. As a black man, I have several white men that I am good friends with. We have helped each other grow and we are all stronger, better men as a result. When considering a friend of a different race ask yourself these questions:

1. Do we think alike? Thinking alike is an important requirement for any relationship.
2. Do we have similar goals? All relationships go through changes. If you have similar goals you will change together for good.
3. Are we both strong enough to be friends in spite of what others may say? There are people who will have negative things to say about you choosing to be friends with someone of a different race. Can you handle that criticism?

America needs a new generation of men who will take an innocent approach toward dealing with different races. Let us strive to be like the five year old who was not pre-programmed about different races but dealt with them based on how they acted.

Wisdom (to be discussed with your mentor)

Understanding leads to acceptance, acceptance leads to influence and influence leads to change.
B. J. TATUM

Prejudice is the child of ignorance. WILLIAM HAZLITT

We hate some persons because we do not know them; and will not know them because we hate them.
CHARLES CALEB COLTON

I don't care where you come from, I want to know where you're going. ANDREW YOUNG

One way to make the world better is by improving yourself. WILLIE WILLIAMS

We must define ourselves by the best that is in us, not the worst that has been done to us. EDWARD LEWIS

People with clenched fists cannot shake hands.
RALPH BUNCHE

Why hate when you could spend your time doing other things? MIRIAM MAKEBA

Kindness is the language that the deaf can hear and the dumb can understand. DESMOND TUTU

Notes:

25. I Will Stay In My Seat
(A Lesson on Concentration)

I remember very clearly the day that it happened. It was a bright summer day in Ms. Spat's fourth grade classroom. I became restless and could not sit still. One of the worst things that I can think of is when I want to go outside or at least get out of my seat and the teacher gives us work to do. Finally I couldn't take it any longer, so I got out of my seat to go to the back of the room. I thought that I would sharpen my pencil because that was as good an excuse as any to get out of my seat. As I went to the back of the room, Mack Hendrix, a kid who sat toward the back of the class, stuck his foot out. When his foot went out, I tripped over it and fell. I made a lot of noise and everybody in the class stopped what they were doing and looked at me. Miss Spat's face turned red and she took me to the office.

While I was in the office, I was supposed to explain to Mr. Thompson (the principal) why I was out of my seat. The real problem was that I did not know why I was out of my seat, other than because I was sick of sitting there. I have always wanted to figure out why I had to get up and sharpen my pencil. Why couldn't I have stayed in my seat? Now that I am grown, I think that I know the answer to these questions.

I think that a lack of concentration is one of the problems that I had when I was young. I always had difficulty thinking about what I was supposed to be thinking about. For example, we had math class at eleven o'clock. It was very difficult for me to think about anything at eleven o'clock because that was just before lunch and the cooks were already cooking the lunch and it smelled sooooooo good.

At two o'clock when we studied science, we were talking about the Apollo spaceship. As soon as we started talking about the spaceship, my imagination would get busy and I would pretend that I was the pilot of the ship and we were gliding through the Milky Way. So, one problem that I had as a kid was that I had difficulty concentrating. If you have this problem, I have some suggestions for you that may help you concentrate.

1. Pretend that you are in a bubble and that the other kids around you are outside of that bubble. This way, you cannot hear them or talk to them. Use this bubble only when you need to get work done. After the work is done, you can deflate the bubble until you need it again.

2. When unwanted thoughts pop into you mind, command them to go away. If they do not go away, determine that you will not listen to them. This is what I learned to do when something frightened me. I would ignore the frightening thoughts and tell my brain to think about my ten-speed bike, my train set, or Gerlene, the prettiest girl in our class. With a little practice, you can tell your mind what to think.

3. Learn to imagine what will happen when you are finished with your project. When the teacher gives you an assignment, always imagine what her response will be when you complete the paper and hand it to her with the right answers to the questions.

4. Think about how you will be able to relax and play after you are finished with the project.
The ability to concentrate is a skill that you must develop if you are to be successful in life. Teachers and other adults can help you learn how to concentrate. Feel free to ask them to help you.

Remember this point. You can always concentrate on the things that interest you. The difficulty comes when we are required to concentrate on things that may not interest us. The smart young man works very hard at developing an interest in things like math, science and other subjects that he is required to study. Telling yourself that you like these subjects will make concentrating on them easier and will result in better grades.

Wisdom (to be discussed with your mentor)

It doesn't matter what you're trying to accomplish. It's all a matter of discipline. . . I was determined to discover what life held for me beyond the inner-city streets. WILMA RUDOLPH

There's nothing mysterious about success. It's the ability to stay mentally locked in. MONTEL WILLIAMS

Each of us must earn our own existence. And how does anyone earn anything? Through perseverance, hard work, and desire. THURGOOD MARSHALL

Nothing is easy to the unwilling. NIKKI GIOVANNI

Concentration is the secret of strength in politics, in war, in trade, in short in all management of human affairs. RALPH WALDO EMMERSON

Thinking is like loving and dying--each of us must do it for himself. JOSIAH ROYCE

We only think when we are confronted with a problem. JOHN DEWEY

If a man sits down to think, he is immediately asked if he has the headache. RALPH WALDO EMERSON

26. Three Kinds of Dumb

When I was a kid, there was a boy in my fifth grade class named Alexander. Alexander was a good kid and we were sorta friends. Alexander was bigger than I was, and I always wanted him to be on my team when we played dodge ball. One thing that always made me sad about Alexander was that he was dumb. What I have learned in life is that there are many ways to be dumb. I know people with Ph.D. degrees who are still dumb in certain ways. My friend Alexander was dumb in three ways.

First of all, he was dumb because nobody could tell him anything. When nobody can tell you anything, you have a problem. If you walked up to Alexander and said: "The bell rang, recess is over and it is time to go inside," he would get mad. I never could understand why he would get mad when you told him something. I think that he just didn't want anybody telling him anything. There are some people who are like that. They just don't want anybody telling them anything at all. Now, to me, that is dumb.

Because of this habit of his, many kids wouldn't talk to Alexander because they did not want him going off on them. When we are dumb in a certain area, we need to work on that area so that we can get better. As we got older, Alexander never did learn to take advice from others and listen to other people. I can look back and see how that really hurt him.

Another way that Alexander was dumb was that he played all of the time. Alexander would throw spit balls across the room while we were taking a test. This was dumb! I was a normal kid and I liked to play, but there are certain times when you really need to be serious. Alexander never knew when that time was because he played all of the time. It was like he was stuck at three years old in this area. I could not get it through his head to stop doing dumb things at the wrong time. Now, I don't want you to think that Alexander was dumb all over. His grades were great, in fact, they were better than mine. This is why I could not understand why he was so dumb in certain areas.

Alexander was dumb in a third way, and that was he did not care about the future. Alexander would goof off when we were facing deadlines. The teacher would tell us that our reports were due on Wednesday and Alexander would wait until Tuesday evening to begin working on his. The future would always catch him unprepared. The future for every kid is adulthood. Smart kids know that unless they die early in a car accident or something that they will grow up. Think about this. Every adult that you see today was once a kid. Time caught up with them and made them adults, and it will happen to you too if you keep living.

Alexander was a normal kid in many ways, but as his friend I remember the three dumb areas that he had.

I was always worried about him in his dumb areas because one major mistake while acting dumb can really get you in trouble. I remember when the teacher caught him throwing spit balls during a test. She took him to the principal's office and he was suspended from school for two days. His parents really got on his case and took away many privileges. Even after all of that, guess what? He came back to school and still threw spit balls. I never could understand Alexander in his dumb areas.

Well, the real deal is that you and I have dumb areas also. I want to advise you never to feel bad about being dumb in a certain area. As long as you work on it, you can get better and soon be strong in that area. If you were to ask your mentor, he would probably tell you that he has some dumb areas too. My dumb area has always been talking too much. My friends have told me about this, and it has gotten me into trouble on many occasions. Once in junior high school, the coach said something to me and I smarted off to him when I should have kept my mouth shut. This was dumb. I have been working on that one dumb area for many years, and I am getting better at it. I am learning to open my mouth and talk when I have something good to say or otherwise keep my mouth shut.

What are your dumb areas? Are you honest with yourself about your dumb areas, or are you the person who says: "There is nothing wrong with me."

All human beings have faults and areas where we need to grow. Listen to your friends and adults who care about you, and they will show you your dumb areas. Once you have identified them, you can begin to work on growing in those areas. I am happy to report that Alexander did grow up and become an adult, and he did learn how to listen to others. He stopped playing all of the time but he still goofs off a little bit.

Wisdom (to be discussed with your mentor)

Everybody is ignorant, only on different subjects.
WILL ROGERS

To be ignorant of one's ignorance is the malady of the ignorant. AMOS BRONSON ALCOTT

There is nothing more frightening than ignorance in action. GOETHE

Your mind is what makes everything else work.
KAREEM ABDUL-JABBAR

All of us are born in a state of ignorance, and many of us never change residence. EFFI BARRY

Some people dream of great accomplishments, while others stay awake and do them. CONSTANCE NEWMAN

The mind is like the stomach. It is not how much you put into it that counts, but how much it digests.
ALBERT JAY NOCK

When I was a boy of fourteen, my father was so ignorant I could hardly stand to have the old man around. But when I got to be twenty-one, I was astonished at how much the old man had learned in seven years. MARK TWAIN

Notes:

27. What I'm Gonna Be When I Grow Up

When I was a kid we lived on the top of a hill, and in order to get downtown we had to walk one mile and catch the bus. As a little boy, I was extremely impressed with the big red bus that would take us downtown. There were several things about the bus which impressed me. First of all, the doors in the back opened and closed by magic (or so I thought). The driver had this BIG steering wheel that clicked when he would turn the bus, and the air brakes made this hissing sound. To me, that bus driver was the coolest man alive and he had the best job in the world.

Most kids choose what they want to be based on what impresses them while they are young. When you are five years old, a big bus, truck, race car or airplane will impress you. When you turn ten years old there are other things that impress you, and by the time you are eighteen years old you have a whole different set of things that impress you. So, when a 5-year-old boy is asked what he wants to be, he will usually choose something that impresses a five-year-old.

What I want you to consider is not what impresses you, but what are you good at. What skill or talent do you have that you do naturally and like to do? Some kids are born with a love for music, math, communicating, dancing, healing, competing, designing, building and many other things. I have always had a love for music. I started playing the guitar when I was in the fifth grade and I grew up and played professionally. I also had an interest in auto mechanics and building houses. I ended up getting a degree in music, teaching school and later becoming a minister.

Most kids have more than one talent or gift. This is good because you *never* know what you will end up doing in life. You may plan to do one thing and end up doing another. You may go to college and train to be a nurse and end up with a career selling houses. The world is changing constantly, and there is no telling what will be in demand fifteen years from now.

In the 1930's a man could make good money playing a saxophone because there was no such thing as a record, cassette or CD. All music was live music. Then they invented the record and people started listening to records instead of going to hear live bands play. This has also happened in more recent years in professions like teaching, law, farming and other professions. So when you think about what you want to be, you had better consider how the world will change in the next 20 years.

One thing that amazes me is how many young boys want to be in the NBA. It is good to dream and I encourage you to dream, but you also must look at the numbers. Very, very few young men will make it to professional sports. You may be one who does make it, but the odds are very much against that. So don't sit back in your seat, look up at adults and say: "I don't have to study because I'm going to play ball for a living." Adults have read the statistics and they realize that the odds are against you. I am not saying that you should not strive for the NBA, but you should have a back-up plan in case you don't make it.

You see, everybody loves the athlete while he is playing. After his playing days are over, it seems like nobody loves him anymore. That's the way it is when a cute young man plays ball. The bad thing is that the cute young man everybody loved will turn into an adult that nobody wants to pay because he can't play any more.

I suggest that you start now reading everything that you can get your hands on so that you will be prepared to do whatever you choose to do when you become 17 years old. Reading is the key, because if you can read, you can learn anything that you want to learn. If you don't read well, you will be hampered as you seek employment.

What do you do well now? What strength do you have in the classroom? Seek to identify your strengths and start exercising them now so that they will be ready when you grow up. If you are good at organizing things, ask the teacher to let you help her organize the classroom materials. If you have leadership abilities, make sure that you take advantage of every opportunity to lead small groups in class. If you are good at handling and counting money, ask to be the treasurer in your school groups.

Once you figure out what you like and are good at, you should begin to work in that area to prepare you for your future job. If you want to see a miserable adult, find one who has to work at a job that he or she does not like. Your working years can be happy, productive years if you begin to prepare for your future job now.

Wisdom (to be discussed with your mentor)

My father taught me how to work; he did not teach me to love it. I never did like to work, and I don't deny it. I'd rather read, tell stories, crack jokes, talk, laugh—anything but work. ABRAHAM LINCOLN

The only place where success comes before work is a dictionary. VIDAL SASSON

I knew I had to make it. I had the determination to go on, and my determination was to be somebody. JAMES BROWN

We make a living by what we get, but we make a life by what we give. BARBARA HARRIS

The best way to develop any career is heart first. MALCOLM-JAMAL WARNER

No task, rightly done is truly private. It is part of the world's work. WOODROW WILSON

The best career advice given to the young is, "Find out what you like doing best and get someone to pay you for doing it." KATHARINE WHITEHORN

If a man will not work, he shall not eat. II THESSALONIANS 3:10

I am only an average man, but, by George, I work harder at it than the average man. THEODORE ROOSEVELT

It is only through labor and painful effort, by grim energy and resolute courage, that we move on to better things. THEODORE ROOSEVELT

Notes:_____

_____

_____

_____

_____

_____

_____

_____

_____

_____

_____

28. The Truth About the Truth

I have always been a pretty obedient child. Most of the time, my mother only had to tell me things once. The reason that she only had to tell me once was that I had learned that mom usually knew what she was doing and she would not tell me wrong. My older brother loved to tell me wrong things, so I always had to question anything that he said.

I guess you could say that my mother told the truth. I learned that the truth would always get me in the end if I disobeyed it. My classic memory about disobeying the truth was the time that my mother told me not to touch the lamp in the living room. You see, we had this old lamp that was coming apart at the top. If you were not careful, it would shock you. Well, I did not listen to my mother and I went to turn the lamp on. I touched the raw metal and immediately 110 volts of electricity flowed through my body, causing my bones to jolt and my teeth to rattle. The shock that I received was a shock of truth.

If you ignore the truth about life and specific things, you are bound to get some shocks in life. My friend Terry would always ignore the truth that his mother told him. When I was a kid, we had to walk a long way to school. On the way, there were two busy streets that we had to cross. Terry's mom told him only to cross the street at the corner while the light was green because it was safer than crossing in the middle of the block.

Well, as you might suspect, Terry did not listen to the truth that his mother shared with him. He proceeded to cross the street in the middle of the block. One sunny day after school, he was hit by a little old lady driving a Cadillac. She did not see him because the sun was shining in her face. Terry was not killed in the accident, but his left knee was crushed and today he walks with a limp in his right leg. This limp reminds him of the truth that he ignored.

Truth can be your best friend or it can be a force in your life that constantly corrects you when you disobey it. You see, it works this way. Truth sits in the middle of the road of life. There is no way to go above , below, or around it. Truth will test the choices that you have made and it will reward you with what you deserve, good or bad.

I can remember a boy in my neighborhood named Raymond. Raymond was a bully who would beat us kids up for no reason. He ignored the truth that if you treated people badly, someone will come along and treat you badly. One day Raymond knocked Jamie's front tooth out for no reason at all. It seemed like every day Raymond was causing someone pain. Well, one morning some people found Raymond in the alley behind the recreation center. He was bleeding badly and later died. Nobody knew who did it or what the motive was, but I heard an old person say that if you treat people badly, someone will treat you badly.

Truth was Raymond's enemy, but I decided early in life to make truth my friend. I know that if you treat people with kindness, kindness will come back to you. When I was younger I owned a truck. I helped a lot of people with my truck and was rarely paid for it. A few years later I sold my truck and moved to another state. I found it interesting that on several occasions when I needed a truck, there was always one available "free of charge." There are many, many other stories I could tell about how I did a good deed and later on truth determined that someone should do a good deed for me.

Well, what about you? Are you doing things that will make truth your friend or will truth repay you with negative consequences a few years from now?

Wisdom (to be discussed with your mentor)

Facts do not cease to exist because they are ignored.
ALDOUS HUXLEY

The truth is cruel, but it can be loved and it makes free those who have loved it. GEORGE SANTAYANA

I don't give them hell. I just tell the truth and they think it is hell. HARRY S. TRUMAN

Pure truth, like pure gold, has been found unfit for circulation because men have discovered that it is far more convenient to adulterate the truth than to refine themselves. CHARLES CALEB COLTON

There's no free lunch. Don't feel entitled to anything you don't sweat and struggle for.
MARIAN WRIGHT EDLEMAN

Truth is the property of no individual but is the treasure of all men. RALPH WALDO EMERSON

Some people handle truth carelessly; others never touch it at all. ANONYMOUS

Get the facts at any price, and hold on tightly to all the good sense you can get. PROVERBS 23:23

29. Peer Pressure

Peer pressure is something that parents have always worried about. When I was a kid, my parents worried about me being affected by peer pressure. Now that I am grown and have kids of my own, I worry about them being exposed to the wrong kind of peer pressure. My kids go to school with many other kids. Some of these kids have not been taught right from wrong. Kids who have not been taught right from wrong may do bad things like have sex at an early age, sell drugs, cuss the teachers and many other bad things.

Now that I am grown, I understand things about peer pressure that I did not understand when I was a kid. One thing that I know now is that not all peer pressure is bad. There are some kids who put positive pressure on others they hang around with. I can remember a kid like this when I was growing up. His name was Charles. Charles was a good kid and everybody liked him. He made good grades and was very confident about who he was and where he wanted to go.

I always admired Charles because he did not let the negative pressure get to him. I never told him that I admired him, I just watched him. I wished that I could walk away from peer pressure and not let it affect me like Charles did. Charles had learned something very important. He had learned how to be peer pressure and not give in to peer pressure. This is the key to success with peer pressure. Learn to be positive peer pressure to the other kids and don't let them be negative peer pressure to you.

You can be positive peer pressure to other kids when you do the following things:
1. Have confidence in who you are and what you want to do in life.
2. Don't be impressed when other people have things that you don't have, such as clothes, fancy hair, good grades, a big house or anything like that.
3. Don't be impressed when other people do things that you don't do such as smoke cigarettes, use foul language, stay out later than they should, experiment with drugs, steal etc.
4. Don't compare yourself to others but compare yourself to the best person that you can possibly be.
5. Strive for perfection in everything that you do.

Learning to be positive peer pressure is one key to becoming a successful person. In order to be positive peer pressure in someone's life, you must have some positive things happening in your life. Nobody is going to be motivated by you when you are not doing your best. It is easy to do wrong, but it is a challenge to do the right thing when others are doing wrong things. Wrong is wrong even if everybody does it and right is right even if nobody does it. Choose to do the right thing even if everybody chooses to do the wrong thing.

Peer pressure can be used as a positive force in your life. It can be used to motivate you to do better. If there is someone in your class who makes better grades than you do, you should try to find out why they are making better grades and use them as positive peer pressure to help you do better. Positive peer pressure is actually someone setting a good example for you. When you observe the good examples around you, do not ignore them. Allow them to motivate you to do better. It is important to resolve to be good peer pressure rather than giving in to bad peer pressure. Kids give in to bad peer pressure for many reasons. Here are a few:

1. They have no plans for their life. If you have not decided where you want to go in life, you can just follow anybody who gets in front of you. If you have plans for your future, then you know whom you should follow to help you get to where you should be.

2. They feel inferior. Many, many young people feel like they are worth less than those around them. It takes very little for some young people to feel inferior. When people feel inferior, they want to feel better about themselves. Hanging out with someone who seems to have his life together usually makes a person who feels inferior feel better. The only problem is that the inferior person begins to act like the person who seems like he has it all together. Often times inferior people imitate people who only have it together on the outside but are falling apart on the inside.

3. They do not have positive friends. Positive friends are very, very important for people who want to do well in life. The reason is that everybody begins to look like and act like the people that they hang around with.

4. They don't have parental support. Because of divorce, absent dads, drugs and many other problems, some boys do not have parents to lead them like they should. When this happens, the young man must decide to do the right thing even if his parents do not help him.

Good peer pressure and bad peer pressure will always be around to hound you. The question is which one you will choose to follow?

Wisdom (to be discussed with your mentor)

I don't know the key to success, but the key to failure is trying to please everybody. BILL COSBY

Learn to see, listen, and think for yourself.
MALCOLM X

A river can't rise beyond its source. What's in the seed determines the fruit. T.M. ALXANDER

Always strive to be more than that which you are, if you wish to obtain that which you are not.
S. B. FULLER

If there is no struggle, there is no progress.
FREDERICK DOUGLASS

If you expect somebody else to guide you, you'll be lost. JAMES EARL JONES

If a man is called to be a street sweeper, he should sweep streets even as Michelangelo painted, or as Beethoven composed music, or as Shakespeare wrote poetry. He should sweep streets so well that all the host of heaven and earth will pause to say, here lived a great street sweeper who did his job well. MARTIN LUTHER KING, JR.

I had heard all kinds of rumors about MIT. They used to say that even the janitors at MIT had master's degrees. At first I wasn't going, but then I couldn't run away from a challenge. I had to compete with the best. RONALD MCNAIR

Notes:_____

_____

_____

_____

_____

_____

_____

_____

_____

_____

_____

Notes:_____

_____

_____

_____

_____

_____

_____

_____

_____

_____

_____

_____

_____

_____

Notes:_____

_____

_____

_____

_____

_____

_____

_____

_____

_____

_____

_____

_____

_____

_____